YOU CAN'T

Drink All Day

IF YOU DON'T START

in the Morning

Also by Celia Rivenbark

Belle Weather

Stop Dressing Your Six-Year-Old Like a Skank

We're Just Like You, Only Prettier

Bless Your Heart, Tramp

YOU CAN'T

Drink All Day

IF YOU DON'T START

in the Morning

Celia Rivenbark

St. Martin's Press ⚎ New York

"The Wrestler and the Fan" originally appeared in
Southern Fried Farce, 2008, Jefferson Press.

Library of Congress Cataloging-in-Publication Data

Rivenbark, Celia.
    You can't drink all day if you don't start in the morning / Celia
Rivenbark. —1st ed.
        p. cm.
    ISBN 978-0-312-36301-7
    1. American wit and humor.   I. Title.
    PN6165.R595 2009
    814'.6–dc22   2009016204

First Edition: September 2009

10   9   8   7   6   5   4   3   2   1

FOR MY DEAR

mother-in-law, Nancy Scott Whisnant,

ONE HELLUVA SOUTHERN COOK

Contents

Contents

YOU CAN'T

Drink All Day

IF YOU DON'T START

in the Morning

1

TB or Not TB: Perfect Attendance Nuts Don't Care

It doesn't win me any points with the other mommies, but I tend to loudly yell *"Booooooo!"* and make lots of exaggerated thumbs-down gestures whenever a kid skips up to the stage to receive a perfect attendance certificate at the end of the school year.

Sure, it's a little unorthodox—some might even say rude—but I don't think it's any ruder than risking everybody else's health just so you can get a stupid fill-in-the-blank award certificate from Office Depot. You know what our little family got for your kid's perfect attendance? The month of March with a scaly rash and violently unpredictable diarrhea.

Well. You asked.

Perfect attendance awards are usually presented at that tasty combo platter that is the year-end assembly, awards presentation, fifth-grade graduation, and nacho bar. It gores my ox every single year. Hence the booing.

"What's *wrong* with you?" asked my fitness-freak mommie friend. I try not to hate her because she always arrives breathless from something called spinning class. For the longest time, I thought she was doing something with yarn but then I found out there's actually a class where all you do is sit in a room and ride a bike that doesn't go anywhere. You need a class for that? How about breathing in and out? Need a class for that, too?

Fitness mommie was pissed at me. She would need to do a few dozen downward-facing dogs and journal for at least an hour to center herself.

"You just booed a *child.* Who does that?"

"Boooooooo!!!" Guess she got her answer.

"Stop it! Those kids are going to get their feelings hurt. Here. Have some edamame. It'll keep your mouth shut."

Fitness mommie is always able to wrestle huge Ziploc bags of edamame from her purse at any given time. I just laugh because I grew up surrounded by soybean fields and hog corn, both utterly useless when faced with actually needing to prepare *food.* But now edamame is every damn where and I am so over it.

As the guidance counselor gave with the left and shook with the right, and the proud kid with the *wet, hacking cough* blew his nose on his shirt and waved happily to the crowd, I turned to "Edda."

"He's a snot factory. Same as the rest of them. Look at

'em. They're so stressed out trying to get that perfect attendance certificate that now half the third grade has fifth disease. If it weren't for kids like him, there probably wouldn't have ever been a first through fourth disease. Hey! Thanks for coming to school with a *hundred-and-three-degree fever, loser!*"

Edda scurried away to find another seat but I just raised my voice. Like a crazy person.

"Look at that woman with the camcorder," I hissed to no one in particular. "Her kid hasn't missed a day in *five years*. I heard his appendix burst one Thursday and she told him 'Don't be such a pussy; that's what weekends are for.'"

The parents drive this craziness, you know. Oh, sure, by about sixth grade, the kid has totally bought into it: Must. Have. Meaningless. Certificate. But it's the parents' fault in the beginning.

I know a woman who got a little brass lapel pin for never missing a day of school all the way through twelfth grade.

"I went to school with *measles,*" she said ruefully one day. "Can you imagine?"

Hell, no! I laid out of school if there was a freakin' wedding on *Another World.* Fortunately, my mother understood this addiction and cheered me on.

"Let me write a note," she'd say.

I usually handled the note-writing because, to my mother, actually laying out of school to see Rachel get married yet again was a perfectly logical excuse.

"No, no!" I'd say. "We can't tell the truth! It needs to be

something really dramatic, something nobody wants to really follow up on."

Fetching notepaper from a kitchen cabinet and plopping into a recliner, I'd compose an entirely respectable letter to the teacher that usually included the phrase "agonizing pain emanating from her females."

(In the South, and perhaps elsewhere, a girl or woman refers to her inner workings as her "females." I have never heard a man call his workings his "males," but it wouldn't bother me particularly.)

Over the years, my friends and I had gotten extremely clever with the writing of sick notes. I like to think it was the start of my professional writing career. Only then, I was paid in Sugar Daddys or Black Cows. Some people are born to greatness; others have it thrust upon them. So it was that most of the dumbasses in my class would come to me for a great sick note. One showed me a note her mother had scribbled.

"Nobody's gonna believe this. It don't even make sense," whined Opal-Anne.

The note was truly awful and, no, it didn't make no sense at all. Written in Opal-Anne's mama's sad little scrawl, it read, "Please accuse Opal from gym class. Her period has done swooped down on her."

From that day forward, I always thought of menstruation as a huge hawk that would dig its wrinkled yellow feet into your scalp for five to seven days a month and just sit there going "Caw! Caw!" or whatever the hell noise hawks make.

My mother's willingness to be a coconspirator on keep-ing me out of school for important weddings of TV charac-ters has carried over to the raising of my own precious cherub, Sophie, who gets much of her own health informa-tion and life guidance from TV, just as her mother did before her. Family traditions are sacred, y'all.

Sophie's getting a crash course on some of this stuff now that the nightly news has informed me that one in four teen-age girls has a sexually transmitted disease.

All together now: "Ewwwww."

Naturally, I summoned the Princess to the TV so she could hear it from Brian Williams' own mouth.

"Mooooommmmm," was the response, accompanied by a big eye roll. "That's gross."

"Indeed it is, little missy," I said.

It's hard to believe my baby is going to middle school in a few weeks. It seems like only yesterday I was lying to kin-dergarten teachers about having to go out of town on busi-ness just so I could avoid having to bake shamrock-shaped cupcakes.

Good times.

And it really *was* just yesterday when the school nurse called to say that the Princess had thrown up during Human Growth and Changes class.

"Some students are just more sensitive than others to these videos," the perky nurse explained as I applied a wet Brawny towel to Soph's pale forehead. "One little boy actu-ally *fainted*."

I looked at the nurse for a few seconds and realized that I should choose my words carefully. I am, after all, a mature adult.

"What kind of perverted shit are y'all showing these kids?"

Yeah. I said it just like that. I'm pretty sure the nurse was considering recommending me for in-school suspension but she knew my lumpy ass would never fit in that tiny desk.

Listen. I happen to believe that schools don't need to be in the business of teaching sex education to children.

That's what TV is for.

Which is why I'm making sure the Princess learns everything she needs to know from a trusted, reliable source that stresses consequences: *One Tree Hill* on the CW network.

It's like Human Growth and Changes, only it has an actual plot and the music is sick!

The Princess and I watch *One Tree Hill* together, which is my own way of educating her about nasty stuff. Sure, it's a slightly unorthodox approach, but *OTH* covers everything she needs to know: the perils of unprotected sex, the perils of drugs, the perils of ignoring the creepy Goth kid, the perils of cheating at love and basketball—it's all there.

Plus it's filmed in my hometown so I'm partial to its addictive charms.

My idea? Ditch Human Growth and Changes and show the *OTH* episode where Nathan had a suspicious discharge. Or maybe that was Brooke. No, it was Rachel. Whatever—you'd be scared straight.

I signed my traumatized Princess out for the day and drove straight home.

I tucked her into bed, gave her a mug of tomato soup with a big crouton in the center, popped in the *Cinderella III* DVD, and promised her that she would never have to see a video about testicles again.

When he got home from work, duh-hubby, naturally, was thrilled to hear that sex education class had made his daughter sick. Men are so predictable.

One thing was for sure. Neither Soph nor the unfortunate little boy who had fainted during the sex-ed video (the little boy whom my husband likes to call "my future son-in-law") would get perfect attendance awards. Not that she was ever in any danger of it.

Back in the assembly, watching the idiot parents fist-bumping and high-fiving was making *me* sick.

I was grateful that I didn't have to go to school with measles, like my friend did all those years ago.

The very word "measles" just scares the shit out of me every time I hear it. I had measles when I was six and remember it being a round-the-clock "itchy and scratchy" show. Plus, it gives you rabbit eyes and the virus means you can contaminate unborn babies and make them come out with extra noses or, worse, as Republicans.

"I can't believe what I went through to get that stupid pin," she said. "My parents were assholes."

OK, that was actually me that said that last part.

Giant, self-absorbed a-holes. Hey! You know where most

of the kids with perfect attendance pins are these days? Me neither!

Harvard doesn't give a shit, I'm guessing. Think about it; you have an award for simply showing up where you were supposed to.

I just read about a Michigan teenager's parents who gave her a new car for having never missed a day of school from kindergarten through senior year. The family told reporters that she made it every day even "despite colds."

Who'd have thought it? Colds in Michigan!

I hear they're spread by being *sneezed on* by sick people who come to school just so they can get a stinkin' Pontiac. And all the edamame in the world isn't going to make you feel better.

Some people swear by chicken soup for a cold but my mama's vegetable-beef soup works best for me and mine.

CURE-WHAT-AILS-YOU VEGETABLE-BEEF SOUP

My friend Susan uses this basic recipe but substitutes 93 percent lean ground beef for the beef stew. Susan is a true friend, arriving with a gallon of soup, a bottle of wine that she bought at an actual wine store, and a box of Sam's Club frozen chocolate éclairs on my doorstep one evening when she heard I was feeling puny. She so rocks.

2 pounds (more or less) beef stew

1 onion, chopped

2 ribs celery, sliced

2 tablespoons olive oil

6 cups beef broth

1 or 2 potatoes, cut into chunks

3 carrots, sliced

5 cups water

1 medium can tomato sauce

2 cans tomatoes

3 teaspoons salt

1 (10-ounce) bag *each* frozen lima beans, corn, cut green beans, and (optional) okra

In large pot, saute beef stew with onion and celery in 2 tablespoons olive oil until beef is browned; drain off nearly all the fat, but leave a little in the pot for flavor. Remove beef, onion, and celery from pot and set aside. Pour broth into the same pot and cook potatoes and carrots a few minutes in the broth until they're softened. Return the beef, onion, and celery to the pot along with water, tomato sauce, tomatoes, salt, and frozen veggies. Simmer for at least a couple of hours; longer is better. In the last 20 minutes, you can throw in some uncooked rice or noodles if you want it to be even heartier. Serve with hot cornbread or saltine crackers if you're pinched for time and drained of energy.

2

Poseable Jesus Meets Poser Ken

In this corner (of Walmart), ladies and gentlemen, a buxom, scantily clad, and heavily made-up Bratz doll complete with poutsome red lips, F-me heels, and tons of "Oh, no you did-unt" attitude.

In this corner (again, of Walmart), ladies and gentlemen, the Prince of Peace himself, the comforter of the poor, lame, and disenfranchised, complete with simple wheat-colored tunic, kind eyes, and gentle demeanor. Yes, folks, it's the Jesus doll!

And here's the kicker! He's a poseable action figure! And why must we always use exclamation marks when we talk about action figures?!

One2Believe's line of biblical action figures includes plenty of familiar faces, although I was a little sad to see there was no tiny tax collector sitting in a tree. I love me some Zaccheus!

Of course, where there are action figures, there are action sets to accompany them and give them depth. So it is actually possible to buy a Moses and the Ten Plagues action kit that comes complete with poseable Moses, stern-looking Pharaoh, and "a bush covered with locusts."

I'm guessing the marketing folks had a real challenge on their hands with that Ten Plagues idea. How exactly do you pitch that product? "Hey, kids! Collect a new pox every week!"

(Little Jimmy, disgustedly: "Criminy! They're out of oozing boils, Mom; I'm going to have to get more frogs falling out of the sky. . . .")

Of course, these days you gotta hold a kid's interest with more than a few smelly store-bought sores. That's why these poseable action dolls talk!

If you press the button on the Moses action figure, he'll bark, "Ye shall not commit adultery!" along with a host of other buzzkill commandments. (Did the Bratz doll just look downward in shame?)

But first: "Ye"?

I totally get that these toys are designed to create one "teachable moment" after another, but they might want to make the dialog a little easier for kids to relate to: "For reals, get outta my grill, Goliath!"

The voice of the Jesus action figure seems all wrong to

me, too. He sounds way too old and angry for someone in his thirties. If this Jesus said, "Let the children come to me, for theirs is the kingdom of heaven," they'd just start shrieking and run to their mommies.

Fortunately, scary-talking Jesus comes with "a unique stop-and-start button" that allows you to pause him, mid-Bible verse, and do something else, say letting the accompanying three-inch-tall lions lick their chops over the frightened Daniel action figure.

Now don't get me wrong. I have nothing against faith-based toys, but these just seem a little too violent. In the promotional materials, Samson and Goliath are shown frozen in a gruesome choke hold, eyes bulging. Gimme that old-time religion, the kind that doesn't involve strangulation.

With toys like this, it's only a matter of time before you hear one Sunday School kid say to his buddy, "My Goliath can kick your Samson's ass!"

Poseable Samson, at just over a foot tall, is the largest Bible action figure. Grotesquely muscular and wearing a post-Delilah modified bob, he comes with a backstory that reminds kids that he "killed a lion with his bare hands, slew thirty men in one night without weapons, and defeated an army of a thousand using only the jawbone of an ass (sold separately)."

You get the distinct feeling that the kindly cucumber "Larry" from the Bible-based "Veggie Tales" series would end up sliced thin and smeared with cream cheese on white bread if he hung around this snarling Goliath too long. Still, I award bonus points for the use of the word "slew."

Shelf space being what it is, there's no telling who Jesus is going to be hanging with in Walmart. Let's hope it's not the new Black Canary Barbie, who is clad in a suitable-for-S&M black vinyl jacket, high-heeled boots, fishnet panty hose, and nothing else.

On the other hand, Jesus was forever befriending loose women, so I guess that would be OK. Picture the inevitable action kit: angry mob (stones sold separately) would have to back away with Jesus in the house.

And it will take nothing short of divine intervention to help shelfmate Ken, long-suffering beau of Barbie.

Not long ago, Ken was given a Mattel "makeover" to try to win his woman back from Blaine, Barbie's vacant-eyed surfer-dude boyfriend.

The makeover was meant to make Ken look more "slick and urban." Speaking through a humanoid working at Mattel, Ken said, "My new look will be very *now*. It will reflect my personality and change with my mood on any given day."

Dude. This is almost as bad as saying "Ye." If you're going to try to reclaim Barbie, you better act fast, am I right, JC?

And he'll probably never have a shot at Black Canary Barbie, who's based on the DC Comics hottie. She's taken to hanging around with another DC superhero, Firestar, whose breasts appear to get bigger as her superpowers engage.

Isn't that *fabulous*?! I'd give anything for my breasts to get bigger when I did something really well. It wouldn't have to be something like shooting star-shaped fireballs straight out of my nipples, although that is wicked cool. But just something more age-appropriate. Like, every time I pull a particularly delicious tuna casserole from the oven, wham-o!

"Oh, these! I get them every time I truly excel at something. Please stand back. I have a praline cheesecake coming in a moment."

Black Canary Barbie looks like the real thing, although Mattel chose to omit her most awesome feature, the "canary cry," a high-powered sonic scream that has the ability to shatter objects and completely incapacitate those around her.

Just like Céline Dion.

Listen up, Ken. Barbie's hot for Blaine, a guy who kills time by picking his toe jam with a coconut husk. If you really want to win her back—and with nearly five decades in the relationship, I don't blame you for trying—you're going to have to man-up.

Ken's handlers say that he's undergone some plastic surgery to resculpt his face. OK, this is so not a good way to start manning up. In fact, it may be the worst start since Michael Jackson decided to wear a military uniform.

If Ken is determined to win Barbie back, it may mean retreating back into the dream house closet, so to speak.

Ken's going to need fewer stylists and more Russell Crowe—the bad boy Russell Crowe who throws phones at innocent hotel employees, not the doting celebrity dad who has, it's official, had his kid surgically grafted to his shoulders. We haven't been this sick of a parent pose since Madonna wore her adopted Malawian orphan bouncing on her hip like a Birkin bag with eyes.

Ken needs to show Barbie that he's willing to take some risks, and I don't mean trying pear-scented maximizing shampoo instead of the usual melon or forcing himself to stop using the word "product" in any conversation about his shaving needs.

Perhaps he could steal Barbie's convertible and run over a few dozen paparazzi. Ken has a lot to learn about image. Angelina Jolie is twice the man he is; then again, so is Dakota Fanning.

Speaking through Mattel, a forlorn Ken has said he'll do anything it takes to win Barbie back. Ick. I can smell the desperation from here. Or maybe that's his Clinique Happy for Men. Either way, *très* unattractive!

If he really wants to win back the vapid vixen, and I have to admit that sometimes I can't imagine why, Ken will need to play hard to get, stop groveling and, trust me, torch those silver lamé chaps he fancies when he's pretending to be Nutcracker Ken.

You think Blaine would wear silver chaps?

Let's ask him.

Oops, too late. It's nine A.M. and he's already passed out in the sand after smokin' his third bowl.

I know what the crew back on the toy shelf is thinking and I hear you: Where's the jawbone of an ass when you really need one? This guy needs slewing.

3

Let's Go See "Gobbler" Up at the Funeral Home

Southern children are just naturally tougher. And if you don't believe me, consider the way my friend Sara used to get to school in the morning. Her grandmother, Miss Edna-Earle, drove a big old Pontiac whose rear passenger-side door would swing open every time she'd make a hard right turn.

Every morning, Sara assumed the position, gathered her books and, as Miss Edna-Earle made her sweeping right turn into the school yard, the back door would fly open and Sara would fall out, landing neatly at the front door. She'd pick herself up, dust off her books, and holler, "Bye, Grand-maw!"

Miss Edna-Earle would then turn a hard left out of the school driveway, the door would slam shut, and she'd toot the horn three times for I Love You.

Southern kids are used to that sort of eccentricity.

Quirky drivers thrive in the South. Growing up in a very small Southern town, we knew that of all the grown-ups we knew, Miss Lou was the most dangerous driver.

She drove a big black Cadillac and was notorious for knocking the doors off cars at the precise moment that you'd be settled behind the steering wheel and reaching for the door handle to shut it.

Truth was, if you were fool enough to park in the Piggly Wiggly parking lot in Wallace, North Carolina, circa 1975, there was a roughly 85 percent chance that your car door would be knocked right off its hinges by Miss Lou before you could shut it and be on your way. She came out of nowhere sometimes, reminding us of that truck in *Duel* that tortured Dennis Weaver or, worse, Stephen King's maniacal Christine.

People in Wallace would just nod understandingly as we drove along, our legs and bodies exposed to the elements until we could get the door put back on at the body shop on the outskirts of town.

The police always gave Miss Lou a ticket, of course, but she was unrepentant, for the most part. That door had gotten in her way. People really ought to be more careful. One time, a Yankee moved to town and, after losing his first car door to Miss Lou, he petitioned the police chief to take her license.

"Well, I can't do that," the chief said. "How would she get around town? She's 'bout six ax handles across so it's highly unlikely that she's going to just walk anywhere she wants to go, now isn't it?"

This is the small-town Southern lawman at his best. If you want to hear about him at his worst, consider the time the deputy encountered a freshly escaped convicted bank robber on the streets.

"Man, you look just like that bank robber that just escaped from the state penitentiary," said the lawman. "Yep. That's the damndest thing. You got the, uhhhh, same eyes. Same hair. Same, let's see here, yep, same skull and crossbones tattoo on your left earlobe. Yep! I'd say you're a humdinger-dead-ringer for that convict."

As the story goes, the escapee's jaw dropped and he waited for the handcuffs and gun to come out in a blur. No point running now.

Instead, the lawman tipped his deputy's hat, said, "Yep, that's quite a co-inky-dinky. Nice day, now," and headed on to his daily lunch of pinto beans and cracklin' cornbread.

When the Yankee was told that Miss Lou needed her license more than he needed his car door, he gave up and eventually moved back up North where, according to him anyway, no one had ever lost a single car door to the same crazy old woman.

What a glorious and strange land that must be!

Many's the time that I've had to explain to someone not from around here why we're such awful drivers in the South.

My theory is that we're so damned tired of being sweet

the rest of the time that we save up all our hatefulness for the relative anonymity of our cars. Southerners are all, "After you, no you, no you first!" until we get behind the wheel.

You blink your turn signal for us to let you into traffic and we just pretend not to see you. Hey, your ass should've left home earlier. You wanna know what your problem is? Poor planning, that's what.

On the road, the average Southern driver takes on a "wouldn't give you air if'n you were trapped in a jug" mentality.

Turn signals? For years, I've told Yankees we don't use them because we know where we're going and it's nobody else's damn business.

We also believe that when it comes to traffic signals, red is the new yellow. Also: the green arrow requires at least a seven-second delayed response 'cause we love to see that little vein pop out on your forehead as you sit and stew behind us.

In the South, at a four-way stop, the rule is simple: The truck with the biggest tires always has the right of way. In the event that there is no truck, just cars, then the right of way always belongs to me. I'm serious.

One more thing: We know we drive too slow in the left lane on the interstate. What can I tell you? That popping vein thing just never gets old. Crazy, I know.

Small Southern towns embrace their crazies, which is something that a lot of "outsiders" can't understand.

My friend Mindi routinely deals with that plague of the

South, the water bug, by shooting at them with a BB gun in her own house.

"It took me seven shots but I got the bastard," she said. "I'd had me a tension headache all day but I want you to know that when I saw his guts splattered across the ceiling, well, bless God, my headache just melted away like butter on a biscuit and I felt like I'd really accomplished something."

To truly appreciate this story, you should understand that Mindi is a college graduate, a professional woman who belongs to the local country club. A lousy aim, though. I'm sure as shit that I could've killed that water bug with three shots, tops.

It speaks volumes that a Southern woman can consider it normal, even commendable, to shoot bugs off her ceiling in broad daylight.

My friend Nina channels the wisdom of her Southern ancestors when her young'uns throw a tantrum. She politely goes to the refrigerator, removes the gallon Tupperware jug of ice water that she keeps handy at all times and pours it on 'em, midtantrum, then tosses them a towel and tells them to clean up their mess.

Everybody's just a half bubble off plumb in the South. Even our crackheads have more personality than most.

Take Skipper and Poo, a local couple who were trying, despite an unfortunate addiction to crack, to have a Norman Rockwellian Thanksgiving dinner with their food-stamp turkey.

At least Poo was. She had just pulled the turkey out of the oven when, like a flash, Skipper snagged the golden-brown bird, tossed it into the basket of his bicycle, and rode two miles to Old Bethel Road to trade it for crack. Witnesses said that Skipper was equal parts afraid of Poo's wrath—she chased him down the road on her own bicycle—and the pack of wild dogs that followed a trail of fragrant, turkey-scented steam wafting on the wind during that unseasonably warm November day.

Redneck Southern women can be fiercely creative when push comes to shove, as it so often does in the rural South.

Flo applied for a job at the bacon plant. She failed the drug test but she had a good reason. The state investigator asked her what she meant by that and she politely and thoroughly explained that a neighbor, whom she didn't really get along with, had recently been arrested for growing marijuana. And, see, her husband, being an avid hunter and having hunting privileges on the property where said marijuana was being cultivated, had killed a deer who, unbeknownst to them as they feasted on venison that evening, must have grazed on the patch of marijuana.

Therefore, Flo had accidentally ingested "pot-meat" and had tested positive. Anyone could see that was perfectly logical.

Then again, this was the same woman who, having failed a drug test the year before, claimed it was because her husband was "a very casual cocaine user" and they had had sex the night before the drug test and obviously he had transmitted the cocaine residue to her through "his bodily fluids infecting me during lovemaking."

If Southern women are just a little bit crazy, it's probably the fault of the men in their lives.

My friend Sarah, who lives in Louisiana, said her first date with her fiancé was memorable because he arrived to pick her up in a red pickup with full camouflage interior and then drove her deep into the woods where he pointed, with tears in his eyes, to a nondescript patch of dirt and said, "That's where I shot my first deer." The gravity of the moment wasn't lost on Sarah who, having older brothers, understood that you wouldn't share such a special moment with a woman unless you were planning to marry her.

In the South, we have more critters than elsewhere and we mingle with them fairly easily.

Most Southern children can recite at least one story involving the witnessing of a frog being swallowed whole by a passing water snake. And if they can't, their ancestry is questioned and possibly ridiculed.

When a Southern child grows up and ventures out into the world, he or she may be puzzled to learn that, in other parts of the country, people usually just have one name and, what's more, might not even have a proper nickname!

Reading an obit the other day in a Mississippi newspaper, I was impressed at how every male family member had a nickname listed. The deceased was "Gobbler"; and his brothers and assorted kin were "Spike," "Hun," "Doots," and "Tiny."

Speaking of obituaries, some newcomers to the South don't understand that when we say we're going to go see so-and-so "up at the funeral home" it means that so-and-so is, well, dead.

My friend Natalie, who is as Southern as hoppin' John with Texas Pete sprinkled all over it, was mortified to realize that she didn't understand that for the longest time.

"Granddaddy would say, 'Well, I'm going to go see Bobby. He's up at the funeral home.'"

It took her years to understand that Bobby, or whomever, was in a pine box up at the funeral home and respects were being paid.

OK, one more thing that all Southern children know, and this may be the single most important advice I can ever give a non-Southern male marrying into a Southern family: Never, ever wash your wife's cast-iron skillet.

Perhaps the saddest note that I have received over the years came from Julie Ann, who married a Yankee man a few years ago.

"On Mother's Day, I got to sleep late, which meant about ten 'til eight," she wrote. "While I was sleeping, just my Mother's Day luck, my husband, who never does any domestic chores whatsoever, decided to get all aim-high and decided to clean the cast-iron skillet I'd left on top of the stove."

Hons, when I read those words, I had to sit down. Because I knew what was coming.

"This was the cast-iron skillet that I got from my great-aunt Connie Jo for my wedding shower ten years ago. It has been lovingly seasoned over the past ten years, having fried enough bacon to clog the arteries of the entire state of Texas. It has made hundreds of servings of fried okra, cornbread for countless holiday meals, gravies too numerous to mention, and our daughter and I made her very first blackberry cobbler together in this pan. It was seasoned to perfection, a gleaming black bottom that I could see my reflection in."

I poured myself a glass of wine to steady my nerves as I continued reading.

"Do you know what my boneheaded Yankee husband did? He came to me, all proud, saying he 'got my old skillet clean, you know, the one with all the crap on it.'"

Julie Ann said she got a little dizzy at this point.

"You mean my *cast-iron* skillet? The one I got for our shower? That one?"

Her duh-hubby just grinned, stupid and proud. "That's the one! It took more than an hour, but I got it clean!"

He had assaulted her skillet with a Chore Boy scrubbing pad, stripping off nearly ten years of perfect seasoning.

Julie Ann began to cry, the great heaving sobs of a Southern woman who has married an ignoramus. He brightened and offered to buy her a new skillet.

And that sums up how Southerners view life and love, y'all. New is not better. Shiny is overrated. These are truths we hold dear in the South, where we embrace imperfection for the gift that it is. Y'all can say "amen" now.

Here's a recipe that I've made in my own lovingly seasoned cast-iron skillet, which I keep in the oven 365 days a year, where Duh will *never* find it.

Sure, you could catch your own crabs down at the dock with some string and a chicken neck or two, but it's OK to cheat and buy it at the fish house. Serve this with shredded slaw and hush puppies. The recipe comes from actor Robert Duvall, who bragged about them on *Oprah* one day many years ago, and I've been making them ever since. When he came to film *Rambling Rose* in our town, I got to interview him for the newspaper. Nice guy, fabulous crabcakes . . .

ROBERT DUVALL'S MAMA'S CRABCAKES

1 pound backfin crabmeat
1 tablespoon mayonnaise (Duke's, if possible)
2 eggs, lightly beaten
½ teaspoon Worcestershire sauce
½ teaspoon cayenne pepper
¼ teaspoon salt
½ onion, grated
½ tablespoon dry mustard

18 Ritz crackers, smashed up (I like to put them
inside a Ziploc bag and then roll over them
with the rolling pin a few times)

Combine everything in a big bowl. Form into six pat-
ties. Fry in enough butter to keep everything from
sticking, over medium-high heat for about 10 minutes
per side. Garnish with lemon and tartar sauce.

4

High School Musical
Triumphs: Dreams 1, Snot 0

s we settled into our seats for the second act of a splashy stage production of Disney's *High School Musical* we'd driven 150 miles to see, I did the math: two mezzanine tickets, plus gas, $140; one oversized peanut-butter cookie and chocolate Dippin' Dots shared in the lobby before the show, $6; one youth medium-size *HSM* T-shirt, $20; sitting among kids and grown-ups who spent the entire two-and-a-half hours obsessively text-messaging and ignoring the show, priceless.

Yes, I get it. You have the attention span of a gnat and rather than enjoying the show, it was *very* important that you tell someone, perhaps even the media, where you were and what you were doing.

Oh! This just in: No one cares.

To tell the truth, I was a little surprised to see the tweens texting their friends. It wasn't like parents were demanding that their kids sit through all eighteen hours of Wagner's *The Ring*, now was it? So, yes, I was a little disappointed that the target audience spent the show staring glassy-eyed at the little blue screens in their palms instead of savoring the real world in front of them.

That said, I accept that kids are put on the planet to confound us and steal our liquor.

My beef's with the grown-ups. If you're bored with what's on stage, why don't you haul your rude butt out into the lobby and text yourself into an exhausted puddle? Text until the paramedics have to come and sew your stupid thumbs back on. But don't pretend you're doing something important. You aren't punching in missile launch codes; you just told your husband to pick up dog food at Costco. You are a moron.

Throughout the play, the woman beside me feverishly text-messaged while her tween looked over her shoulder to read, giggle, and offer (in a loud, annoying whisper) suggestions for other people to text. They were so cool. They were at the *HSM* stage show. Except they weren't. The woman was well into her forties and was letting her kid know that (a) performers really don't deserve attention or respect after months of rehearsals and (b) I repeat, she was a moron.

This wasn't Broadway, but that was lucky for the audience, the way I saw it. If you pulled this junk in New York, they'd toss you out of the theater and onto 42nd Street before you even had a chance to pretend you were just checking on your dying grandma.

I'm a little sensitive, maybe, about all things *high school musical*. If you must know, I have such an awesome crush on Zac Efron. Not in some creepy Mary Kay Letourneau let-me-have-your-baby-you-man-boy way, but in an isn't-he-a-nice-young-man kind of way.

In fact, I have an awesome crush on the entire cast and so do many of my "mom" friends.

If we really want to piss off our daughters, we gently stroke the *HSM* messenger bags on the rounder at Limited Too and say, a tad too loudly, "Ohmigod, could Corbin Bleu *be* any cuter?"

So, when tickets for the traveling musical went on sale I got in line quick. Good thing, too. Dirtball ticket scalpers have gotten good at getting blocks of seats at all the tween events.

Remember how they grabbed up all the Miley Cyrus/Hannah Montana tour tickets? They didn't even know who she was but that didn't matter. All they knew was her tour was selling out faster than (awesome and inappropriate crush of '04) Justin Timberlake and (short-lived crush of '94, ruined when I heard him refer to his bossy wife as his, ick, soul mate) Sting.

So while normal and admittedly unsophisticated moms and dads naively waited their turn to buy tickets on the day they were released, scalpers must've been laughing their criminal asses off at such futility. Fools!

Oh, sure, a few would be successful (even a broken clock is right twice a day, didn't someone once tell you that back in juvie?), but not many, on account of the fact that scalpers have computer programs that help them jam phone lines and buy up huge blocks of seats at every venue, then resell that $67 ticket for many times that amount. Suckas!

Of course, it's not all the scalpers' fault. One nut-job parent paid more than $2,500 so his kid could see Miley Cyrus. Hell, I wouldn't pay $2,500 to see George Clooney at my door toting a case of Pinot Noir from his own vineyards and hankerin' to talk to a woman of substance for a change.

So I get that we spoil our kids these days, keeping the mangy scalpers in business. But $2,500? As Miley's alter ego, Hannah Montana, might say: "Scum-sucking greed-monger charged *what*?"

But there were happy times ahead for the mommies and me. The *HSM* sequel was finally coming on the Disney Channel. I knew this because I had put big *X*s on the days counting down to it on my "The Many Moods of Zac Efron" wall calendar.

"Omigod, can you believe we almost didn't TiVo it?" said one mom friend before making the dreaded *L*-for-loser shape in the air above her forehead.

"Nobody does that anymore, Mom," huffed her mortified ten-year-old.

"Of course they don't, honey!" said the mom, brightly. "I believe you . . . *not!*"

"They don't do that either, Mom."

"As if."

"Or that."

Gawd.

I'm not sure this has ever happened before. How to describe it? Well, it's as if it's 1964 and your parents are standing in front of their black-and-white Zenith screaming and crying because the Beatles are appearing on *The Ed Sullivan Show* and you're a tween who's yawning and asking them to let you know when the ventriloquist with the singing monkey comes on.

Oh, don't get me wrong. Kids like *HSM,* even the boy kids.

But moms *love* it, perhaps because it's a little bit *Grease,* a little bit *Footloose*, and a whole lotta retro goodness.

High School Musical makes us feel young and hopeful again. I'm fairly certain that even Disney, which has its corporate finger on the pulse of tweens to the point that they must surely feel light-headed most of the time, didn't even expect this.

Middle-aged parents jogging with "Stick to the Status Quo" and "Bop to the Top" on their iPods? How did *that* happen?

Maybe this is my generation's overdue optimism finally kicking in.

Face it, we grew up listening to Jethro Tull describe homeless pedophile Aqualung as a snot factory with an unnatural attraction to little girls. Compare and contrast this with the ebullient *HSM* lyrics, which simply invite everyone to join hands together in making all their dreams come true.

Final score: dreams 1, snot 0.

Sure, it's simpleminded fluff, but every now and then, when you've had a shitty day at work and a fight with your best friend, and you've got eight loads of laundry to do, a little fluff makes a mighty soft landing at the end of the day.

HSM isn't the only trend that adults have practically taken over from their kids. If your coworker asks you if you'd like to see his "love puppy," or tells you he's got one "cheeky monkey," don't call him a perv; he's just addicted to Webkinz, stuffed animals that have an online identity that requires you to feed, entertain, and generally take care of them. Or else.

It's hardly news that kids love Webkinz. But now the parents are hooked.

Look around; your coworkers might be angling for "magic forest charm bracelets" instead of Xeroxing their butts or playing computer solitaire like in the good old days.

"You gotta keep 'em well, happy, and healthy," a mom friend explained with utter seriousness.

When her kids went to sleepaway camp this summer, she spent hours making sure that the many demands of their ten Webkinz were taken care of.

It's like real life, only it's not.

Last week, while my kid checked on the food dish for her virtual pet and contemplated how much "KinzCash" she'd need to buy a virtual swimming pool, her seven-month-old kitten was rolling on the floor below her, slowly and dramatically choking on a three-inch blade of grass that had somehow gotten lodged in her nostril.

"Hell-o!" I said, pointing to the kitten, now trying to give herself a tiny Heimlich maneuver with her own little forepaws. "Real life happening over here!"

(Since you ask, it cost one hundred bucks to sedate kitty and remove what I now call the World's Most Expensive Blade of Grass. I have placed it in a little shadow box like it was one of those face-of-Jesus grilled-cheese sandwiches or something.)

While neglected Webkinz don't exactly die some horrible *Meerkat Manor* kind of death (screw you, Animal Planet, for letting Flower die!), they do get the dreaded Webkinz "green snout" or clutch tiny ice bags to their virtual heads when they're not well tended.

The only way to get a sick Webkinz well again is to take quizzes or perform jobs that earn KinzCash so you can buy medicine for this virtual pet that, remember now, is actually based on a smallish stuffed animal sitting on your kid's dresser.

That's just shoot-your-preacher-husband-dead-then-demand-custody-of-your-kids crazy, isn't it?

Across the country, people of the male persuasion are

shirking office work to play Webkinz games online instead of shirking office work to study their fantasy football team's stats like God and nature intended.

Username Fluffydad is worried about his ailing Sherbet Bunny. It's the beginning of the end, y'all.

5

Miss North Carolina Is
Too Nice to Hate

Aside from too many cute guys calling me "ma'am," my reign as the North Carolina Pecan Harvest Festival queen was, in a word that I just now made up, Pecan-TASTIC!

My lifelong dream of riding on a float and doing the demure "unscrew the lightbulb" wave was finally realized. I cut ribbons, I extolled the virtues of the pecan, I walked around for two whole days with a crown pinned to my head, I had breakfast with Miss North Carolina at our pecan-TASTIC B and B.

Miss North Carolina, Jessica Jacobs, is slim and tall and gorgeous. As we chatted, just the two of us, she dined on a small compote of fresh fruit and a dainty cup of herbal tea. I, on the other hand, had three eggs, homemade sausage, toast, juice, two of those compotes, a hunk of blueberry-oat coffee cake, fried potatoes, and coffee.

I'm fairly certain Miss North Carolina has never, as I did, leaned over to anyone and asked, "Are you gonna finish that?"

As we sat in matching tiaras at the breakfast table, I was struck by how queenly she was. I had much to learn. I also had butter on my chin.

I had borrowed three fur jackets to choose from, so I asked Miss North Carolina to tell me which one looked best with my consignment-store steal of an evening gown.

"Oh, the white one, definitely the white," she said.

"Are you just saying that or is that a beauty pageant trick like where you tell another contestant they look perfect and really they've tucked the back of their dress into their panty hose by accident?"

Miss North Carolina looked hurt. Great. The mean old lady had hurt Miss North Carolina's feelings.

During the Pecan Harvest parade lineup later that morning I got to meet my "queen's court," seven cute and bouncy high school girls.

"How did you get this gig?" I asked the nearest one, a sweet thing named Madison.

"I had to write an essay about how much I wanted to represent my town because I really wanted to give back to the community that has given so much to me."

"No, quit shittin' me. Really, how'd you get this gig?"

OK, that's what I was dying to say because all that sincerity was starting to make my eggs come up. Besides, I'd been told these girls would serve me. Not a stinkin' one of them had so much as offered to detail my car. These girls had a lot to learn about servitude.

As queen, I was on the last float, just like Santa is in the Christmas parades. Which was fine since, after that breakfast, we were roughly the same dimensions. The float snaked through the tidy streets of Whiteville, North Carolina (yes, its real name). Small children scampered ahead, trying to grab all the candy tossed by the firemen who had preceded us.

"Get out of the way!" I called cheerfully.

Somewhere Miss North Carolina was cringing on the back of a convertible and thinking that I have a lot to learn about being royalty, even for a weekend.

The journey had been fun, though. When they first approached me to be queen, I reminded them that, despite a very flattering picture on my Web site, I am not nineteen or even close. Plus, I wasn't really pageant-ready. My thighs got more dimples than Jeff Probst and I can actually find Rwanda on a map. That's two strikes right there.

Y'all know I have issues with beauty pageants but this was different. The Pecan Festival queen committee actually wanted its choice to be a bit of a hag. They didn't say that but they did say "seasoned," which is the same thing.

Having turned fifty just as the invitation to be queen arrived, I have to admit it sounded like just the shot in the flabby upper arm that I needed.

Frankly, until the queen committee called, I'd been feeling a little down. It hadn't helped when, at my favorite grocery store just a few days earlier, the cashier had said, while I swiped my debit card, "Don't worry! I took off the senior discount."

"Whaaaa?"

Apparently convinced that I was both old *and* deaf, he smiled even wider and said, quite loudly, *"I said, I deducted the senior citizen discount for you. It's Tuesday, you know. You get five percent off!"*

What can I tell you? The room began to swim. Yes, there was prune juice in the cart, but that wasn't for me. And what if it was? Prune is the new plum.

"How old do you think I am?" I asked through clenched, and now that I thought about it, somewhat loose teeth.

"What?" he asked, still grinning foolishly and not quite understanding the out-of-nowhere raging can of whup ass that was gonna be opened up on him.

"I said, *How old do you think I am?*"

Finally, the slow dawn of recognition crossed his lineless face. Other shoppers paused to listen in.

"Oh, I-I-I-I'm sorry," he stammered.

But it just wasn't enough. A primer on manners was in order. Primer, now that I thought about it, sounded like a very old word.

"You should never, ever assume a woman is a certain age; it's rude," I said. Besides, I was wearing $45 foundation and day-old highlights. Clearly, this asshole was blind.

The bagger, a sweet elderly fellow, having missed all of this horror, approached with his own goofy smile.

"Ma'am, do you need some help with these bags?" he asked.

OK, it was official. I was fifty and decrepit, unable to carry two grocery bags out of the store without collapsing.

While the cashier fervently tried to catch the eye of the bagger and shook his head *no*! quite violently, the bagger bored in on me, eyeing me from head to toe.

"Ah, tough day at work, eh?"

Holy mother of God! Would this never end? I grabbed my bottle of Pinot Grigio before he could hide it away in its embarrassed little paper bag. Perhaps I would smash it on the counter and drink from its ragged neck, here and now.

"No, not a tough day at work. Actually, I have to go pick up my ten-year-old at school now."

"You got a ten-year-old?!" was the incredulous response from the bagger. Meanwhile, the cashier was on the verge of tears.

"Yes! And right now I'm having a happy period despite my advanced age and clear addiction to prune juice and cheap wine. Go freakin' figure!"

After that late unpleasantness, being a queen would be the perfect antidote.

It was weird turning fifty. When I grumbled to friends, they said, "Sure beats the alternative!"

Yes. I know that. If this was 1906, I'd have been dead at least ten years from childbirth or horse pox or something equally gross. Then again, without movies-on-demand, it wasn't like I'd be missing all that much.

Would turning fifty mean that I'd start behaving

strangely? And by that I mean ordering fried shrimp and drinking it with hot coffee and then complaining about how the coffee's never hot enough?

My friends scoffed at my anxiety and said dumb things like, "Fifty is the new forty!" Which just made me realize that there are a whole lot of other people who suck at math as bad as I do. No. Fifty is fifty. And overall, I'll take it over horse pox any day.

It was thrilling to be asked to be queen of anything at my age. These people *got* it. Age means wisdom!

In preparation for the big weekend, I memorized many pecan facts. Did you know, for example, that there are more than a thousand varieties of pecans? Personally I only recognize one: the kind that goes in my stomach. I adore pecans, and that has nothing to do with the many pounds of shelled halves that found their way into the trunk of my car.

Pecans are not cheap, my hons. In fact, in the South, the street value of shelled pecans just before holiday baking season is roughly that of crack cocaine. Do not confuse the two. It is almost impossible to make a decent crack cocaine tassie, I am told.

In my research—I was going to be the smart queen—I learned that "pecan" is a Native American word which, translated from the Algonquin language, means "This is gonna make Stuckey's a lot of wampum some day." Would the Pecan Festival queen lie to you?

Riding on the float that chilly November morning, I felt the years melt away.

It helped a little, too, when Dan Rather, along about the same time, said that he thought Katie Couric would "tart up" the nightly news.

Katie Couric, the fifty-year-old tart! The notion that a woman our age could be a goofy sexpot was, frankly, refreshing. Granted, "tart" isn't the kind of word you'd find in the urban dictionary denoting unrelenting coolness. To some, the reference was so dated they didn't understand he wasn't talking about a pastry. Nope, this tart was a hussy, a real strumpet!

Of course, Rather was chastised and had to issue a P.C. retraction saying that Couric wasn't a tart but was, in actuality, a respected journalist.

Oh blah, blah, blah.

The whole thing reminded me of a scene in HBO's fabulous *Six Feet Under*. Kathy Bates was a middle-aged shoplifter who never worried about getting caught.

"Don't worry," she told her friend. "They don't even see you. It's as if we aren't even here."

It was brilliant but depressing. I've noticed that when shopping in the cool stores, the wee, tiny salesclerks seldom offer to help me. I am invisible at fifty. Many times, however, they will run themselves ragged trying to assist their own tiny kind.

So, yes, it's fun to think you could still be a tart—or a

queen—at fifty. Beats being the invisible drone buying her teenager's underwear and begging someone to wait on her while thinking maybe it wouldn't be so hard to just stuff it in her purse and walk on out . . . to get some coffee, good and hot.

Now here's something wonderful from the N.C. Pecan Harvest Festival queen's friend Mabel to try with that hot coffee. This pecan pie isn't as cloyingly sweet or as rich as some. Try it sometime.

If you're showing off for the circle meeting, be sure to top each slice with a generous dollop of freshly whipped cream and a dusting of cinnamon. If you must use the canned stuff, remember—it makes a racket coming out of that nozzle thing so you'll need to turn up the radio preacher so the ladies won't realize you're fixing to serve them whipped cream out of a can.

PECAN PIE FIT FOR A QUEEN

½ cup sugar
1 tablespoon all-purpose flour
2 eggs
1 cup light Karo syrup
¼ teaspoon salt
1½ teaspoons vanilla extract
1 tablespoon butter, melted
1 cup pecan halves
1 unbaked pie shell

Preheat oven to 300 degrees. Sift sugar and flour together. Beat together eggs, syrup, salt, vanilla, and melted butter and add to mixture. Pour into unbaked pie shell. Arrange pecan halves in a pretty pattern on top. Bake for about an hour. Cool completely before cutting or it'll be a royal mess.

6

My Manservant Can Kick Your Ass

The woman watching me wash my hands in the restaurant's restroom approached with a look of amused curiosity.

"May I ask you a question?"

"Sure," I said, figuring she was going to ask if I knew that fewer than half of the bathroom-going public washes its hands and that she couldn't help noticing that I actually wash my hands while singing the "Happy Birthday" song twice in my head like I read somewhere you're supposed to. Then again, how could she know that? Who was this woman and where did she get her eerie thought-reading powers?

The woman cleared her throat and looked me up and down.

"I'm visiting from California and I can't figure something out about you people who live here."

For a second or two, I wondered how she could be so sure I was a "local" but then I remembered that she had probably overheard me instruct the Princess to "See can't you find us somewhere to dry our hands since this paper towel thingy's all mommixed up."

Yes, that might have been the tip-off.

"Go ahead," I said, plastering my best "Welcome to the South" smile on my face.

"Why is it that the women here don't have a tan? I mean, you people live on the coast. What's going on?"

OK, that was twice she'd said "you people," which is just one of those phrases that, no matter how innocently spoken, always sounds condescending.

She was plenty tan, this woman, and I felt like Casper McWhitelady standing beside her.

Her question blindsided me. So I said the first thing I could think of, which was the truth.

"Southern women hate wrinkles and skin cancer."

No applause necessary, Chamber of Commerce; I am here to serve.

Where did this come from? I sounded as fun-loving as mildew. Would someone, anyone, please remove the stick from my ass?

I had committed the unpardonable sin of being rude to visitors because Ms. California was brown as a nut and I was telling her that (a) she was gonna die and (b) she'd probably die ugly.

So I tried to make up.

"Of course, that's not to say that you would have those problems," I said, oozing in Southern charm. "I'm sure the California sun is much less, uh, sunny."

"No, not really," she said. "Sun's sun. I just think it's weird that you people are all so pale."

Oops, a third "you people." All bets are now off.

"We people," I said slowly, "need to be pale; otherwise how would you detect our red necks?"

"Good point," she said.

"I was being sarcastic."

"Oh. That's cute."

Cute. Why was I letting this woman get to me? If she wanted her skin to look and feel like a pita chip, that was certainly her business, bless her heart.

Much is written about Catholic guilt and Jewish mother guilt, but I think Southern daughter guilt is the worst of all. We are raised to make sure everyone around us is comfortable, happy, included. I had failed miserably with this woman.

Southern men are raised to be polite. At least most of them are. Occasionally, there are unfortunate exceptions.

I'm thinking about the man I observed leaning against a Sun Drop cooler in a convenience store recently who was yelling loudly enough to wake the dead or, in this case, the store clerk whose head jerked up when he heard the commotion.

"Hey!" the man was shouting. "Don't you got eyes? Can't you see all these people waiting in line?"

I felt terribly sorry for whoever was getting yelled at. The restroom was occupied so I stepped back and waited to hear the sound of the useless hand-dryer gizmo. It wouldn't be long now.

Suddenly, I felt that electrical charge in the air that you always hear people describe right before a tornado hits.

My hair stood on end. On a nearby rack, the Slim Jims appeared to be combusting in their little red and yellow jackets.

Yep. There was a lot of tension up in here.

I looked around, discreetly of course, to see who had cut in line, but everyone was staring back at *me*!

Oh, shit.

Yes, despite the fact that the yelling man, along with a woman who appeared to have the tremendous misfortune to be romantically aligned with him, and four fidgety children were a good twenty feet from the restroom door, I had broken in line.

"Are you addressing me?" Yeah, I said it just like that.

Addressing. Who *says* that? What was next? Was I going to invite him to engage in a battle of fisticuffs with my husband and his manservant?

Maybe it was the foot-long turkey drumsticks smoldering in their glass case a few feet away, but I felt the urge to go medieval on this guy.

Never in my life has a man yelled at me like that. I don't

want to sound like Mrs. Drysdale but the truth is, a Southern man never raises his voice to a woman he doesn't know, especially one who is just the teensiest bit older than he.

It simply is not done.

Besides, it was hard to understand how a person could basically stand on the shoulder of the interstate and expect me to deduce that he and his litter were in line for the facilities.

"Yeah, I'm talking to you."

"I'm so sorry," I said, sweetness oozing from me like a stomped-on Twinkie.

Which, now that I think about it, I was.

"Are these precious cherubs yours?" I asked, backing away from the restroom door.

"Do what?"

"These here your young'uns?"

"Yeah. And they need to pee."

I wanted to tell him they might want to stand a little closer to the toilet owing to his family's odd distance-perception problem, but that would've sounded vaguely snotty.

What had happened to this Southern man? Had he been raised by wolves, or worse, the French?

I decided that I could make it another forty-five miles to the next rest stop, so I power-walked back to the car, head held high.

"Make haste!" I hissed at my husband.

"What's wrong?" said Duh. "You didn't get to go to the bathroom?"

"Why would you ask that? Could it be because I'm sitting

here crossing my legs tight enough to crack walnuts between my thighs?"

"Yeah. Something like that."

I told him the whole sorry story, embellishing it a bit from the safety of the car.

Southern women are, frankly, "bad to embellish," as Aunt Ovalene would say. You can be "bad to" anything; just fill in the blank, although it's mostly used as "bad to drink" to describe a relative's disappointing alcoholism.

"He was very threatening in his demeanor," I said.

"You sound like the way they talk on *Law and Order*."

"Nonsense. I haven't used the word 'perp' in a sentence, maybe, ever."

I fear that Southern mamas aren't teaching their sons "how to do" anymore, and it's disgraceful. Rather, we are raising a regionful of, well, perps.

Witness the young man who slouched unhelpfully at the shoe store when I took the Princess shopping for back-to-school.

"Excuse me. Could you help us?" I asked.

"With what?" he drawled, all eighteen and full of attitude and Doritos breath.

OK. Wasn't expecting that response. Then again, he was young and it probably wasn't his dream job to peddle kids' shoes to middle-aged women, no matter how attractive I might be.

"My daughter needs some new tennis shoes. Can you recommend a brand?"

"Over there."

OK, this wasn't going well at all. This chile had no raisin'.

"Over there" didn't even come with a wave of the hand. Still, as my Sunday School teacher Beth always says, you never know what another person is going through on a particular day, how tough his walk might be at that moment.

At least a dozen times a day in traffic, I fight the urge to cuss somebody by fantasizing that he or she is driving like a complete asshole because he is so distracted from having just been diagnosed with "the cancer." Actually, if that was true, roughly 95 percent of my fellow drivers would be terminally ill by my estimation. That's how much they suck at driving.

So, in my mind, I tried to give this rude boy the benefit of the doubt.

I smiled wider, this time through gritted teeth, Garfield-like.

"Over where?"

Huge heavy sigh and irritated glare.

Could I *be* any more of a nuisance?

"You lookin' for kids' shoes, right? They're over there under the sign that says KIDS' SHOES."

Ohhhhhh. So it's like that. Suddenly I didn't care how tough his walk was. In fact, if I could arrange it, he might never walk again.

Soph knew what was coming and began to back away from me very slowly, the same way you'd do if you saw a rattlesnake in your path.

"I see the sign," I said, steely but still smiling. "What I was hoping for was some guidance. Are there brands that perform better? Is there one you'd recommend?"

"Depends on what you want."

"What I want is some customer service," I said, mentally adding "you little shit" at the end of the sentence.

"Say what?"

"Customer service. You know. Like how when a customer comes in and asks you to help them, you make sure that if you can't answer the question, you'll find someone who can and you'll be cheerful throughout the process. Real basic stuff like that."

I felt like Andy Rooney, without all the eyebrows.

"Look, the brands are all different. Depends on what you want. I guess you're just gonna have to let her try some on."

"Are you sure about that?" I asked. "Because, usually we just buy shoes without trying them on because it's just too much trouble to take off socks and untie laces and all that."

Blank stare.

By this time, Soph had found the shoes she wanted on her own. She tried them on and they fit perfectly. We headed to the cash register to pay. Part of me was irked that I was even giving money to this store, but most of me was thrilled that we could check something off our list.

"Was someone helping you?" asked the clerk without looking up.

She must've been kidding.

7

Playing "the Bingo" with A-Cissy and A-Bobby

I took my mama to the Senior Center the other day to play "the bingo." The words are spoken with such reverence in senior circles. It's never "bingo." It is "*the* bingo," rather like certain country folk who still say "the Walmart" and "the Kmart."

I like the bingo, but historically, it hasn't liked me back. No matter. I fetched us a couple of cards and we sat in padded folding chairs at a card table with two Yankee ladies who were clearly regulars.

Not five minutes into the game, I hollered "Bingo!" but one of the ladies at our table leaned over and told me that she was afraid I didn't have "a good bingo."

How could this be? Wasn't my bingo as good as the next person's?

"Not a good bingo," the caller said matter-of-factly into

the microphone after verifying my humiliatingly premature bingo.

Très embarrassing! I slumped in my seat and could read the minds of the other players.

"Thought she had a good bingo. Can you imagine?!"

The caller went back to start another game, never failing to pronounce the number twenty-two as "toot toot," like a train whistle. It was funny the first five or six times.

"She didn't have a good bingo," I heard the woman at the next table say to her friend while nodding in my direction. "Not good at all." God, wouldja let it go already?

On the other hand, the relief that play could continue, thanks to my superbad bingo, was almost palpable.

How was I to know they were playing "the letter *L*" game? Afterward, I was much more careful, finally squealing when I successfully won a flashlight in "the letter *X*" game, my first win ever at bingo.

Afterward, my mama and I enjoyed a very nice turkey and mashed potato lunch for a buck fifty. It occurred to me as I was describing the lunch to my husband later that hanging around my new peeps had changed my speech a bit.

Seniors always describe food in such terms as "I had a nice Oreo with some very nice milk today."

It's a little *Cuckoo's Nest* sounding but harmless enough.

As my mama and I were leaving, our former seatmate said, "Psssst" and pointed at me. I walked over.

In a whisper that told me that, for whatever reason, she had warmed to us and wanted to do something nice, she told me that the Moose Lodge across town had free bingo and chicken salad sandwiches every fourth Thursday if we were interested.

"It's a nice chicken salad," she said. "They don't use too much mayonnaise."

I smiled at her. "From your mouth to God's ears," I heard myself say. Whoa. Where did that come from? I was one week of senior bingo from saying that I sure loved "that a-Cissy and a-Bobby" on PBS reruns of *The Lawrence Welk Show*.

On the way out again, I noticed a poster on the wall announcing that Tuesday was corned beef and cabbage day. There was even a festive note at the bottom with a little flowered asterisk that promised "Sadie's bringing the soda bread!"

I don't know who the hell Sadie is but I am all in on corned beef and cabbage day. It is one of my favorites. Although sometimes cabbage does give me gas if it's not cooked long enough.

Strangely, my mom wasn't nearly as sold on all this as I was, and this was a problem since I needed her to be my "old people's lunch beard," so to speak.

Yes, I was only a distressingly few years away from full eligibility to play and dine, but that might as well be a million years when you see the chance of $1.50 quiche and salad (beverage included!) slip between your fat fingers.

"Can't we go back today?" I whined one Wednesday. "It's corn chowder day and Sadie's making the cornbread."

"I dunno," my mom said. "It's OK, but I don't want to miss my stories."

"It's just one story," I said. "It's *The Young and the Restless,* and we all know that Victor is going to spend at least the next two months chewing the scenery over his dead trophy wife and cutting himself. So! Who wants chowder?!"

"No, I'm not in the mood," she said, settling in for another hour with Victor and company. "You go ahead and tell me all about it."

"Ack! With the complaining!" I said, and flicked the air with my hand like I'd seen Sadie do a dozen times by now. You can learn a few things from these transplanted Yankees, for sure.

"Well then, go to the school. I'm sure Soph would love for you to eat with her class." She was pushing me toward the door with a broom handle at this point.

"Some beard you are!" I pouted. "Oy vey!"

The truth was that since the stock market crashed, taking with it our savings, Soph's college fund and, most important of all, my supersecret Dollywood vacation fund, I had been rethinking eating with my kid every so often at school.

Frankly, the school lunches were $3 for adults and you didn't even get bingo or a beverage. Screw that.

Plus, at the senior center, they let you talk. At Soph's school, often as not, we were subjected to something horrible called "silent lunch," which is just the most unnatural thing in the whole world. You can't ask kids not to talk during lunch. The last time I went, we were all subjected to the dreaded "silent lunch" because one little boy in the class had pooted that morning and then bragged about it.

"You mean we're sitting here not able to even say 'Pass the pseudo honey-mustard sauce that contains neither honey nor mustard' just because that kid over there farted?"

"Yeah," said Soph. "And stop talking. You're just going to make it worse." I felt like we were in Oz—the HBO maximum-security prison, not the Technicolor place with the weird paving job.

The next day, I was back at the Senior Center, playing the bingo and winning yet another flashlight. Prizes weren't as good as when we'd first started going and it was either the flashlight or a can of Del Monte fruit cocktail—no sugar added, so really, what the hell was the point?

Although winning was fun, it wasn't the highlight of the day. No, no. That came when I returned our bingo cards back to a plastic box and the sweet old man collecting the cards looked up at me from his wheelchair and grinned.

"You know somethin'?" he said with a twinkle in his eyes. "You look just like Meg Ryan!"

"Thanks!" I said, practically curtseying and wondering if it would sound braggy if I told him that lately I'd been getting more Marg Helgenberger.

"Don't get too excited," muttered his lady friend. "He's legally blind, you know."

Oh, snap! I wasn't sure if she was doing the circle-and-spray over her man or if she was just being real with me, but I admired her either way.

Besides, I should've figured he was vision impaired when

I noticed he always played on a special card the size of a yoga mat.

Still, it was a sweet thing for him to say and I treasured it. Almost as much as my two flashlights.

A VERY NICE CHICKEN SALAD, I PROMISE!

3–4 cups cooked chicken, cubed

1 cup chopped celery

1 tablespoon minced onion

1 can sliced water chestnuts

1 small jar pimientos

1 cup chopped fresh mushrooms

1 cup mayonnaise (Duke's, if possible)

1 tablespoon lemon juice

1 teaspoon lemon pepper

Topping:

½ cup slivered almonds

1½ cups Pepperidge Farm CornBread Stuffing
mix

Mix everything together in a big bowl and pour into a greased casserole dish. Add almonds to stuffing mix and toss around a bit. Pour on top of chicken salad and bake for about 30 minutes at 350 degrees, covered.

Note: This fabulous chicken salad comes from my friend Mabel Halterman, who knows her way around the Senior Center and used to live across the street from me. Mabel was one of ten children and she learned how to cook when she was just a sprout growing up in rural Sampson County, North Carolina. She said to remind y'all that this chicken salad is good hot or cold. Serve it with some fresh snap beans and sliced tomatoes in the summer.

8

Airlines Serving Up
One Hot Mess

Flight attendant: "Good morning, everyone, and welcome aboard OneHotMess Airlines! We hope you'll enjoy your flight today. In the meantime, those of you who opted for the additional thirty-dollar surcharge for seats with thirty-eight inches of pitch, please relax and enjoy your flight. For the rest of you, well, may God have mercy on your souls."

Pilot: "Yes, good morning from the flight deck. This is your captain speaking and I want to welcome you aboard. It looks as if we'll enjoy a beautiful flight with clear skies and stunning views. As we approach the Grand Canyon, those of you who opted for window seats at an additional five dollars will be allowed to see it. The rest of you must pinky-swear promise to close your eyes or risk the additional ten-dollar late "sign-up-and-see" fee. Sneak peekers risk having their retinas removed by the beefy undercover air marshal presently sitting in seat 4A. Do not mess with him. He once made Steven Seagal cry like a wussy little girl. Really. He did.

"Here at OneHotMess, we not only charge for every checked bag, we also charge $25 for each purse, murse, briefcase, laptop, iPod, and any other portable electronic device you may have brought on board. Additionally, if you are seated in an exit row, you will not only be asked to read the special instructions but also to help push the beverage cart up the aisle as needed. We know that you didn't volunteer for that row because you give a shit about being helpful in a crash, but that you do like the extra six inches of leg room, so don't get all haughty.

"If you are found to be acting haughty anyway, you will be assessed an additional $50 surcharge for 'being kind of an asshole' on the flight. Also, if you are traveling pregnant, or 'TP,' as we say in the industry, please be advised that you will be assessed a fee for smuggling a second passenger on board. At OneHotMess, we do not condone seat-sharing and you will be charged accordingly if you have a recognizable bump. If, upon inspection, we determine that you are not actually pregnant but are, rather, just another victim of too many Applebee's sizzling blond brownies or a cirrhotic liver, we will cheerfully apologize while at the same time inform you that your extra weight will result in the same fee as if it were a carry-on bag. You also will not be offered any of the delicious snacks that are customarily offered to our thinner passengers. They are saving fuel; you are not."

Flight attendant: "Ladies and gentlemen, if you are traveling with small children, please make sure that you have purchased an oxygen mask for them as well. Here at One-HotMess Airlines we recognize that children can be incredibly annoying in general and particularly so on an airplane, and we believe that a lack of oxygen exacerbates this. In a moment, Trixie, the world's oldest flight attendant, will shuffle her tired ass up the aisle and collect your oxygen-mask money. Please note that the mask itself is rented for $15. The tubing through which said oxygen moves is an additional $15. We suggest that you rent both pieces because they are useless by themselves and will only lead your entire Orlando-based flight crew to double over laughing as you try to gasp air through a mask attached to, well, nothing."

"Furthermore, at this time, Trixie will be selling seat belts for 75¢ but, please note, in the event of turbulence, that rate will be adjusted to $35."

Passenger: "May I have an airsick bag? All these add-on fees have made me a bit queasy."

Flight attendant: "I'm so sorry. Airsick bags are no longer on board because our suddenly-enviro-conscious CEO has decided that they are made of paper and paper comes from trees and therefore, we have stopped providing them so we can go green! Rather like your face. Hmmmm. Here! Use my purse."

Passenger: "Oh, I couldn't . . ."

Flight attendant: "Sure you could! Everybody does!"

Passenger: "So that going green thing must be why there is no in-flight magazine?"

Flight attendant: "And they said you looked dumber than a box of hammers when you boarded. You're right!"

Passenger: "But what about the SkyMall? How will I be able to order the putting green that doubles as a cappuccino maker?"

Flight attendant: "Sir, from now on, you will have to buy your overpriced, weird crap from late-night infomercials just like everybody else."

Pilot: "Ladies and gentlemen, from the flight deck, I'd like you all to look out on the right side of the airplane and wave to our special OneHotMess Airline priority platinum passengers who have chosen to avoid the dreaded 'free' middle seat by simply strapping themselves to the wing. Give 'em a wave, everyone! My wife is out there right now. Hang on, Love Dump. . . . We're expecting some gnarly tailwinds today. Folks, at OneHotMess Airlines, we don't have so-called buddy passes for friends and family because, well, that shit costs money. So whenever our friends and family hit us up for discounted or free airfare, we just strap their cheap asses to the wings and most of them arrive alive. Frostbitten, hypothermic, and barely breathing, but alive!

"Ladies and gentlemen, in a moment flight attendants will be dimming the cabin lights so that you will be unable to read any book or magazine you may have brought aboard.

Flight attendants will be coming through the cabin with an assortment of barely used blankets and pillows for those of you who would like a nice snooze during our flight."

Passenger: "OK, I'd like a blanket and pillow, please."

Flight attendant: "Certainly! That will be $40."

Passenger: "Whaaa?"

Flight attendant: "We no longer loan these; you must buy them."

Passenger: "Buy them? What am I going to do with a blanket and pillow once I get off the airplane?"

Flight attendant: "Are you familiar with the phrase, 'Daddy, what'd you bring me'?"

Passenger: "Well, of course, but this isn't exactly a Webkinz. All this price gouging is nuts! Next thing you know, you'll be charging me to complain!"

Flight attendant: "We *so* didn't think of that. Thanks! And have a great flight to Vegas!"

Passenger: "But I'm going to Seattle!"

Flight attendant: "You big silly! That's way farther. Here at OneHotMess Airlines, we tell you where to go!"

Passenger: "Right back at you. . . ."

Flight attendant: "Was that a threat? Was it? Don't make me call you-know-who in 4A. He will kick your priority gold ass all over this airplane, do you hear me?"

Passenger: "I have to go to the bathroom."

Flight attendant: "Say please."

Passenger: "What?"

Flight attendant: "Did I stutter?"

Passenger: "Please. I need to go to the bathroom. Does that cost extra, too?"

Pilot: "Ladies and gentlemen, from the flight deck, I forgot to mention earlier that we have installed pay toilets. You will need $1.87 cents in exact change for each visit to the lavatory. It's a really annoying amount, we know, but it cuts down on the number of trips. Here at OneHotMess Airlines, we're sick of you always jumping up and trying to go to the bathroom just as the beverage service begins. Sit your ass down and wait. You should have gone before you boarded."

Flight attendant: "Ladies and gentlemen, in just a few minutes we will be coming through the cabin with a complimentary beverage service and light snacks. And by 'light' I mean 'imaginary.'"

Trixie: "Y'all, this is Trixie and I just want to say that we understand that the airlines aren't like they used to be and that flying isn't the pleasurable experience it once was. But it's no picnic for us, either.

"Maybe you read about those two skanks that got escorted off a plane after creating a ruckus on a flight last year. These two little swamp sluts said they were mistreated because they were prettier than the other people on the plane.

"I know what you're thinking. It's always the same old story. Unattractive people always get all the breaks, and if there's one segment of our population that's consistently mistreated and abused, it's the fabulous-looking eighteen-year-old girl.

"Passengers, I've dealt with a lot of creeps on the job, but these two? The worst. Dumb and Dumber whined as soon as they got on board a full plane. They wanted water. I mean before takeoff, while the middle-aged bald guy with eczema was still trying to stuff his crappy *Sports Illustrated* duffel into the overhead bin.

"These coach-class bitches cussed everybody out and said the only reason they got picked on was because they were better looking than everybody else on the plane.

"They behaved so bad that when *Daddy Day Care* came on, people actually watched it just to drown 'em out.

"So, as you can see, while we know that the airline industry has made some missteps, it's no picnic working with y'all, either, with your nonstop complaints: 'I can't breathe!' 'This cabin isn't pressurized!' 'There's spooge on my pillow!'"

Pilot: "Whoa, Trixie, that's enough. Passengers, I'm sorry about that little outburst. Sometimes Trix gets a little confused when she takes too many Xanax. I've done the same thing dozens of times. In fact, I just took a handful of those bastards a few minutes ago 'cause there was a guy who looked a *lot* like Samuel L. Jackson getting on board with a box with holes punched in it and I started to freak out a little. But now, I'm mellow. And I'm just gonna take a little nap now. . . . This bird can practically fly itself anyway. Thank God, 'cause I really need some shut-eye. Crap, Trixie, get me another pillow."

9

Gladys Kravitz Would've Loved Her Some Facebook

I guess I should've paid more attention when the Princess and her little friend asked if they could create a Facebook page for me.

"Sure," I said, completely distracted by watching the new next-door neighbors move in that day. They were young. I'm talking practically embryonic. I couldn't imagine how they could even lift all those heavy boxes with those little arm-buds of theirs.

"So it's OK?" Soph asked. "We can put you on Facebook?" She was upstairs and, rather than walk the eight steps to the landing, she was screaming. I screamed back: "Yeah, sure, whatever!" and went back to my perch at the front window.

Oh, gawd. They were standing on the sidewalk in front of the house *kissing*. I couldn't tell them to get a room because, in point of fact, they'd just gotten about twelve of 'em.

"Mommie, what's your star sign?" Again with the shout-ing.

"OK, honey, Mommie is doing some very important re-search right now, so why don't you just fill out the Face-a-ma-call-it and let me know when it's done, OK?"

"OK," she and her pal said in unison. Then they both giggled for a long time, but I wasn't sure why.

From my living room couch, I chewed on a Slim Jim and watched the embryonic new neighbor couple continue to work, toting box after box into their new home—the home beside the crazy lady who watches their every move while eating salted beef ears.

Every so often, the he-neighbor would step aside so she could take her box inside. So cute. What's this? They just dropped boxes and hugged. This move is going to take for-frikkin-ever. I would need more jerky, that much was certain.

After an hour of this I was beginning to get bored, but rather than actually check on my daughter and her friend as they launched my lumpy ass into cyberspace, I decided to take a break and read the magazine beside me on the couch. Great. Oprah's started a new diet where she lives off noth-ing but flaxseed tea and cardboard toilet paper rolls. I threw the magazine onto the floor and went back to spying.

I felt a little like Gladys Kravitz, the chinless, nasally, nosy neighbor in the old *Bewitched* episodes.

These new neighbors, with their youth and their still

slightly webbed hands, didn't know from Gladys Kravitz. If I even laughingly compared myself to her when I finally showed up at their door with my famous "welcome to the neighborhood, now I dare you to ever take a normal dump again" eight-cheese casserole, they'd think it was perhaps Lenny's mother, but even that was a stretch.

"Mommie, what would you say are your special interests?"

"At this moment, spying on our new neighbors," I hollered back.

"Got it!" they said in unison.

"No! I was just kidding. Don't put that!"

I wasn't sure how Facebook was going to look but it was buying me time. As long as Soph and her friend stayed busy with that, they wouldn't be asking me what they could do and I wouldn't have to launch into my "When I was your age, we made our own drugs—er—fun" speech.

Holy God, was that a couch from This End Up? I needed binoculars.

More hugs, another kiss and, now, him lifting her off her feet and looking up at her while she placed her hands on his shoulders and looked down at him. Where had I seen this before? Ah, yes! The movie poster for *The Notebook*. Crappy book, decent movie—am I right?

Things were suspiciously quiet upstairs, but I didn't care. They were happy, I was happy and, God knows, the Notebookers were happy.

I was sure he was telling her that she was the most beautiful woman in the world as he wiped a bead of sweat (dew!) from her sweet, young face, barely missing her ear gills.

And that made me think of Diane Lane, who has acted in plenty of Notebooky movies herself and who must have it written into her movie contracts that her leading man must say, at least once, "You are the most beautiful woman I have ever known."

No, really. Watch for it. It's practically a drinking game. I'm sure Richard Gere even wonders about it. In *Nights in Rodanthe,* I think he just said, "You are the most beautiful, ah, blech, blech, blech!"

The Notebookers continued to move in an assortment of furniture and appliances, pausing for little love pecks every few boxes. As they huffed a stackable washer-dryer onto a hand truck, I waited for her to scream, "Asswipe! Why are you too cheap to hire somebody to do this? I'm gonna bust an ovary over here," as I had done during that exact same scene years ago.

But, no. They just cheered each other on. I gave 'em two years tops.

"Mommie! We finished your page!" I heard, and so I decided to take a look. The moving show was getting boring, even with wine, and I really needed to check on the girls.

But the adorable new couple next door rang the doorbell right about then, cheerfully wanting to borrow a screwdriver and introduce themselves, and I got distracted from

Facebook. In fact, I didn't think about it again for about a week.

That's when I got my first request by an old friend to be allowed into my Facebook world, where our friendship would be viewed by others and become an exceedingly shallow brand of friendship given to four-word sentences and the passing back and forth of lots of something called "lil green patches."

Anyway, I let him in with a quick cut-and-paste, and then a few more crept in. What did it matter? But one day, a "friend" commented rather inappropriately about my marital status.

I finally took the time to actually look at my Facebook home page, and there it was.

Under "special interests and hobbies" was one word: *men*!

I summoned the Princess to the office where my computer lives and, apparently, flirts scandalously with near strangers when I'm not downloading even more constipatory casserole recipes from cooks.com.

"What is *this*?" I shrieked. "My special interests are *men*?! Won't Daddy be surprised to see *that*? What do you have to say for yourself, little missy?"

Sophie hung her head, but not for long.

"Hey, wait a minute! It's not my fault. Remember when we asked you for special interests and you said you were too busy watching the new neighbors?"

"Well, yes, but . . ."

"And when we asked again you said that right then your special interest was wondering why it is that Ashlee Simpson's husband looks exactly like her?"

"OK, but you know I have a curious mind and sometimes, well, journalism is hard."

"But we tried to get you to look at the page before we finished it," Soph whined. She could see that long-promised trip to the mall to go to Forever-a-21-Year-Old-Skank disappear before her very eyes. "We didn't mean to say that you were interested in men like that. We just meant that you're straight."

She was teary-eyed, so I believed that it was a simple mistake and I had her correct it immediately to read that my special interest was "celebrating the human spirit and bringing all peoples of all nations together."

There. That sounded much better.

The Princess then showed me around the site, explaining that I had already been "superpoked" quite a few times.

"That's disgusting," I said.

"No, it just means hello," Soph assured me. Hmmmm. I still had an image of Jodie Foster on a pool table in *The Accused*, but that's just the kind of sick pup I really am. I didn't want to be superpoked by anybody.

I also had a "past-life invitation" from some woman I don't know, who said she could ask me five questions and discover who I was in a previous existence.

There were all sorts of "earthkeeper" invitations, where you send virtual plants to one another and somehow this is supposed to save the planet. Like I care.

There were even "virtual deliveries" of doughnuts and sweet tea, which just pissed me off. What good is a virtual food product? I mean, unless you're on Oprah's new diet.

I also discovered that there were many people who were asking to be my Facebook "friend" and I hadn't answered them yet. I pictured an angry mob of old high school buddies who would grow bitter if I didn't let them in immediately.

"Who does she think she is?" I imagined they would pout, all the while saying how incredibly rude it is to ignore someone's "invitation to knighthood."

My friend Amy, who runs her own business, wastes hours every day reading posts from old friends and sending them invitations to join "I love the '80s" or "virtual bookshelf" or requests for "knock-me-out drinks."

As for me, the only thing I've participated in is the past-life invitation, and let's just say it's pretty hard to be humble ever since I learned that I used to be Eleanor Roosevelt. Who looked a lot like Gladys Kravitz, now that I think about it.

Absolutely everyone has a Facebook page these days. One day over the backyard fence, my adorable child-neighbors asked me if I was on Facebook because, naturally, they are. I told them yes and now we've let one another into our lives via the "interweb." I call it that just to mess with their heads.

"You should be friends with my mom," he-neighbor said one day while planting a rosebush in honor of their (gag) second wedding anniversary. "Y'all have a lot in common. You both look a little like Diane Lane."

OK, so perhaps I was hasty. This couple is actually quite wonderful. And they're growing on me like a lil green patch.

Try this fabulous Southern creation the next time you need to impress the new Yankee neighbors. It's practically vegetarian, give or take a half-pound of bacon, and comes from my mama-in-law, Nancy Whisnant, by way of her late sister Alice Armfield.

NANCY AND ALICE'S "HOWDY NEIGHBOR" PEPPERS

Make the biscuits yourself if you're not too triflin'. And don't even think about using canned tomatoes or substituting chicken broth for bacon grease. This is the real deal, Gomer; don't screw it up.

6–8 bell peppers
½ pound bacon, fried crisp and crumbled (save drippings!)
6 tomatoes from somebody's garden, peeled and chopped
1 bar Cracker Barrel sharp cheddar cheese, grated
¼ cup chopped onion
8–10 day-old biscuits, crumbled
Salt and pepper to taste

Cut peppers in half and parboil them 'til they're softened up but not mushy, about 10 minutes. Drain; set aside. Combine all the rest of the ingredients in a big bowl and add about 4 tablespoons of bacon drippings (OK, grease) 'til things are moist but not mushy. Form into balls and stuff the peppers with this fabulous mixture. Set the filled peppers in a shallow pan and add water to cover the bottom of the pan so your pepper bottoms don't scorch. Bake at 325 for about 20 minutes or until lightly browned on top.

10

Gwyneth Paltrow Wants to Improve Your Pathetic Life

Oh, poor little ol' Gwyneth Paltrow, she of the porcelain skin, pale blond hair, and lithe body. Why on earth would I feel sorry for her? Simple. Because her decision to launch a lifestyle Web site, Goop.com, shows a lapse of good judgment that we haven't seen since a certain cruise ship made its maiden voyage straight into an iceberg.

We know what she was thinking: "If Oprah can make a fortune showing people how to live their lives, why can't I?"

Oh, Gwynnie, where to begin?

For starters, you can't tell people how to live when you're married to a *rock star*. It is, well, unseemly. Oprah's never quite gotten it right in the romance department or the yo-yo dieting department, so we can relate to her a bit better. Also, it doesn't hurt that she grew up ringworm levels of poor in Mississippi.

But you? You! With your adorable *rock star* spouse who is both cute *and* deep and your curiously named but nonetheless precious children, you just can't. Again: unseemly.

The earlier Titanic metaphor is appropriate because Gwyneth is, so to speak, the first-class passenger wearing furs and a brooch the size of Kansas and the rest of us are wearing flour-sack knickers and eating turkey feet down in steerage.

Gwynnie's Web site shares her "life-changing" advice to (oops, here comes my lunch) "pause before reacting," "nourish what is real," "go to a city you've never been to," and, you're gonna love this, "not be lazy."

Oh, heavenly pearls of wisdom from someone who grew up in relentless, soul-crushing privilege, who attended only private schools and who even dated Brad Pitt for three years. We wish we could pause before reacting to the insane high-handedness of Goop.com.

I've read better advice in the headlines of *Cosmo,* which at least offers useful information like "1,001 Erogenous Zones That You Didn't Know He Had! But He—Wink!—Wishes You Did."

On Goop, Gwyneth tells us to "Cook a meal for someone you love."

Hey, Rapunzel, it's called dinner and we do it seven nights a week without, I must add, the assistance of nannies, butlers, and assorted cooks and pot scrubbers.

Gwyneth says that she has a great life because she is "not passive about it," which implies that we are. Guilty as charged, I suppose. I was going to be less passive about life and "shed-yule" my own tour of lesser-known Tuscan vineyards but it was my night to bring snacks to children's choir. My freakin' bad.

Gwyneth Paltrow is telling us not to be lazy? Well. We'll try not to be lazy. And we will try to refrain from pointing out possible signs of her own laziness, such as her dropping out of college or how chef pal Mario Batali has admitted it takes a lot to roust her out of the trailer in time to start shooting their über-trendy food-and-wine adventure show.

I'm guessing Gwynnie's not really a morning person, so it's wonderful that she needs only to arise when she is good and damn ready. One pictures bluebirds flying through her windows and draping her in the day's couture.

Could I be wrong about this? Could goop.com be the answer to our nation's collective angst? Will Gwyneth save our sorry souls with advice such as "Clean out your space"? Maybe. I think I'll start cleaning out my space by taking my *Shallow Hal* DVD to Goodwill. There. I feel better already!

Sure, Gwyneth could be the next Martha. I mean, anything's possible in a world where there are still some people who claim they were shocked when Clay Aiken came out.

I suspect Gwyneth just got some colossally bad advice at a dinner party one evening. Someone must've leaned in and said, "M'dear, you are a marvelous hostess. Why don't you create a Web site where you can tell everyone how to live like you do?"

And Gwyneth, piddling about between projects, must've

thought that was a terrific idea, a way of "giving back," so to speak, without the lifelong commitment of, say, adopting a motherless Malawian boy like her BFF Madonna.

I'm picturing the two taking one of their endless strolls through the rain in London and discussing how Gwyneth could launch her lifestyle Web site for the masses. (By the way, I can't wait 'til that Malawian kid gets enough about him to sit up and say, "Hey, white lady, the photo ops are great but could you just *get my ass out of the rain?*")

I'm sure Gwynnie was advised by her pals on exactly how to save the world one mouse click at a time, but . . .

See, here's the thing: Out here in the world of two-hundred-thread-count sheets and twenty-fifth anniversary dinners celebrated at Olive Garden, Gwyneth's advice seems a bit, well, preachy and weird.

There's a slight finger-pointing tone to her tips, a metaphorical pursing of the lips. We're all just a bunch of big sillies! What is wrong with us?! Life is fabulous and we need to go about the business of celebrating it.

It's kind of like how another rich lady, Christie Brinkley, wanted us in her corner as she slogged through her third very public divorce, but we just yawned.

People get divorced and have custody disputes every day. Christie didn't seem to get that the stuff she was claiming made her so outstanding was stuff we all do.

My heart broke a little when she showed up at the courthouse clutching a dinosaur diorama she'd helped her kid make as evidence that she was a good mother.

What did she expect the judge to say?

"I see that you have helped your child construct a prehistoric animal habitat entirely from Elmer's glue and old newspapers. I believe that my work here is done. You get the kids, the house, the cars, the boats, and all the money."

Why do women always think they have to resort to crafts to prove that they're good mommies?

Will Madonna herself have to drag out her Creative Memories scrapbooks and curvy cropping scissors to prove her devotion to parenting when she finally battles what's-his-face in court?

So we're to believe that Gwyneth cooks every night and Christie helps her kids with their schoolwork? Not bloody likely.

I would've had much more respect for Christie if she'd left Dino in the car and said, straight up: "Your Honor, my husband cheated on me repeatedly *and* he's addicted to Internet porn."

Seems like that should have been enough.

Christie's scuzzy ex, Peter Cook, could have fought back by bragging about how he helped the kids with math homework.

"Your Honor, I always help the kids with their math problems," he could've said. "I tell 'em, if a hooker charges five hundred dollars for thirty minutes and she has three friends who charge one-third of that for twice as long, how much money would you need to have with you or risk getting repeatedly kicked in the nut sack by their pimp?

"Or, how about this? Court documents reveal that Daddy spends approximately three thousand dollars a month on cyber porn. How many polar bears stranded on that melting ice floe that makes Sharon Lawrence cry in the World Wildlife Fund commercial could Daddy save just by giving up his addiction to Adult Friend Finder for six months?"

But Peter Cook did none of that, even as evidence mounted that he was a bad dad, even dunking his stepdaughter's head in a bucket of water. (Frankly, I can't imagine the girl's bio dad, Billy Joel, not calling on old Allentown friend "Knuckles" to deal with Cook, and by deal with I mean causing him to bleed from many new and different orifices.)

For all this misbehavior, there was one thing that cemented, in my mind anyway, that Peter Cook was a jerk: He gave his eighteen-year-old mistress money to buy a Nissan Maxima.

Man, being the mistress of a millionaire sure ain't the gig it used to be. What, were they all out of Dodge Neons?

Given her penchant for advice-giving, Gwyneth Paltrow could have counseled the entire Cook-Brinkley family because, to hear her tell it, she understands the human animal, and I am not just talking about David Duchovny. She admits that she has made a few mistakes, but that was all in the past. Now it's time to share with others what it has taken her a lifetime to learn.

Like—and I am not making this up—"where to eat when you're in London."

Oh, for shit's sake, Blondie, most of us are just lucky to get to Six Flags once every five years. London?

Giving Gwyneth the benefit of the doubt, I will just assume that she got bored with hearing how fabulous her husband was and she's "acting out" rather than just accepting her position as an in-demand and much-lauded actress.

Maybe Goop really got its start after someone desperately tried to keep Gwyneth from becoming the next (God rest her soul) Linda McCartney or (egads!) Yoko.

Chris Martin is insanely talented and the last thing he needs is wifey standing waifishly at stage left shaking a tambourine or insisting on taking the mic during set breaks to deliver a heartfelt plea to save the endangered truffle or whatnot.

This whole business reminds me that women don't know how to be rich anymore. I mean nobody except Heather Mills McCartney who, I'm sure, doesn't cook, unless it is to lightly braise the still-beating heart of a freshly slaughtered baby lamb.

In their attempt to just be one of us—be it through cooking shows, Web sites, or gluing their regal hands together making dinosaur habitats—they succeed only in pissing us off.

Billy Joel (see above) trotted out his latest wife a while back to promote her cookbook. The wife of the world's wealthiest comedian, Jerry Seinfeld, also wrote a cookbook.

It almost makes me like Heather. Say what you will but

Heather Mills McCartney earned her money the old-fashioned way: Marrying a billionaire and then ensuring that his life is so miserable that he'll pay you $43 million just to leave. Write a cookbook? Oh, hell no.

I can hear a few of you out there whining a bit as you read this. After all, doesn't a woman have a right to pursue her own hopes and dreams and talents?

Right. So the tiny, itsy wittle Ms. Joel demonstrated her awesome cooking talents by making meatloaf on Oprah's show.

Yes, meatloaf.

At the mention of meatloaf, the audience squealed as if she'd started to prepare pheasant de foie gras snootypants.

"She's making meatloaf!!!!" Oprah bellowed; you know how she does. And then she bellowed it three more times.

All this is going on and I'm thinking, *Dude, you married Billy F-ing Joel. Fry the guy a steak at least, or make what I'd make if I were married to him. That's right: reservations.*

From all appearances, Mrs. Billy Joel is utterly charming. Ditto Mrs. Seinfeld. But I'd like 'em a lot better if they just sat up there on Oprah's couch and said, "You know what? My husband's worth $800 million. I got no flippin' idea where the stove is. Ewwww. This sofa's sorta scratchy, O."

I guess celebrity isn't what it used to be. Jennifer Lopez and Nicole Richie, in separate *People* interviews, recounted tales of sleepless nights and numerous diaper changes.

Oh, big deal. Celebrities can do poo just like some damn

Appalachian Juno. As if. My guess is, Carmelita is the only one changing nappies in those mansions. What's next? Yard saling with Eva Longoria Parker?

Acting poor is just so 1995, y'all. At least Gwyneth got that part right. Bless her heart.

11

Jon & Kate Plus 8
Better Without the Kids

Have you seen *Jon & Kate Plus 8*, the reality TV show about a Pennsylvania couple who are raising one set of twins *and* sextuplets? While I would've been tempted to just name them Dopey, Sneezy, Grumpy, et cetera, as they kept popping out, Jon and Kate Gosselin aren't the frivolous type.

What fascinates—and repels at the same time—is the couple's weird dynamic: She kvetches and finishes his sentences; he walks around in a semistupor fretting about his workout regimen or his teeth-whitening progress or where they should go on vacation.

While most fans claim to love this show because of the rambunctious, adorable Gosselin children, I just fast-forward the TiVo through all the boring kid scenes.

Any time I sniff a *looooong* scene of eight kids eating Chee-rios for breakfast, I just go "boo-boop" to get to Jon and Kate chatting on the couch. Until those kids are old enough to discuss the environmental impact of offshore drilling or at least have a mature, intelligent discussion about whether or not Zac Efron is gay, I will speed through the endless "Ball! My ball!" arguments, thank you very much.

In each episode, Jon and Kate spend a fair amount of screen time sitting on a cramped love seat facing an anony-mous interviewer and nudging each other in the ribs (a little too hard, I think) and bantering about their chaotic life as the parents of multiples.

A bit player in this psycho drama is Aunt Jodi, a slightly anorexic-looking young mom of four with a penchant for clothes that have that distressing "I buy all my clothes from the TV" Quacker Factory vibe to them. Jodi once agreed to take care of the eight little Gosselins—six of whom *had the flu*—while Jon and Kate flew to California so Jon could get hair plugs.

When Jon got home and complained how much his scalp hurt, Jodi would've been within her rights to carve him up like a Christmas ham on the spot, but she is way too nice to do that.

Another bit is Kate's unfortunate obsessive-compulsive disorder. Watching her yell at the workmen for installing new blinds incorrectly, as in a tiny fraction off center, was downright uncomfortable. Kate is very big on "If you want something done right, do it yourself." Just ask Jon, who hasn't been able to do anything right in Kate's eyes in a very long time, possibly ever.

We'd feel sorry for him if he wasn't such a self-absorbed schmoe, surfing the Web while Kate cooks endless organic meals and scrubs imaginary dust from the baseboards.

If only she'd let him finish a sentence.

Jon: "We were going to go—"

Kate: "To the park, but there was a piece of dried bubble gum on the underside of one of the picnic benches, so I said we should skedaddle to the museum—"

Jon: "Is skedaddle really a word?"

Kate (giggling): "Shut up, you moron (jabs Jon in the ribs 'til blood spurts out of his mouth).

Ratings gold, my hons, ratings gold.

Of course, I'm more than a little concerned now that I hear the Gosselins were so charmed by a vacation to my home state that they've decided to move here, probably adding at least a couple of electoral votes upon arrival.

Because they're partial to North Carolina beaches, where I live, there's no doubt in my mind that they'll pile into the maxivan and cruise two hours east several times a year from their new Carolina home. All eight *adorable* children will spill onto the sand and basically take up every square inch.

"Beach ball!"

"My beach ball!"

And what's this? Aunt Jodi following along wearing her Quacker Factory bathing suit and schlepping all eight little Gosselin floaty rafts?

Kate will spend the entire day at the beach arranging and rearranging the chairs until they line up perfectly and screeching at Jon to stop feeding the gulls because it makes them "go all poopie!"

This is what happens when you're trapped in a house with eight kids all day. You use phrases like "go all poopie" and you use a weird little singsongy voice.

Eventually, the Gosselins will probably become the Singing Gosselins even if none of them can actually sing, because this is what very large families with impossibly cute children must do. There will be a Christmas special and they will eventually make everyone forget the formerly Most Precocious Multiples, the McCaughey septuplets of Iowa, once and for all.

As the CDs of *A Gosselin Christmas* sell in the millions, I can picture a gleeful Kate looking at a photo of the McCaughey family and saying, "Face bitch!"

The McCaugheys have chosen to keep a much lower profile, choosing only annual chats with the perpetually sad-eyed Ann Curry on *Dateline* and the occasional *Ladies Home Journal* update.

Will Jon have to assume the role of Jackson Five patriarch Joe, herding them into the recording studio and demanding that they rehearse until their tiny vocal cords snap like dry twigs?

"Holy God, it's 'TEN LADIES DANCING.' How many times do I gotta tell you? Oh my God, I am so stressed out. Kate, can you handle this? I'm just gonna go grab a tan."

At times like this, OK, at times like when I'm simply breathing in and out, I am grateful not to have eight children.

My grandmother had eight children, spaced out every couple of years or so to assure a steady supply of strong arms and legs to work on the family farm.

Some of us just weren't intended to have more than one child. We can't all be Kate Gosselin—or my grandmother, for that matter.

Members of the one-and-done club can be ferociously protective of that one little cub, though.

That's why I could never understand why the mama of that little Chinese girl who had to sing behind a curtain at the Olympics didn't make a stink.

In the words of Mr. T., I pity the fool that would tell me that my daughter would sing on the sly while the cuter kid would lip-synch and soak up the credit.

Here's the way that conversation would've gone if little Yang Peiyi's mama had, say, just returned from a few months visiting her long-lost adopted sister raised in the Deep South.

Chinese Politburo member (CPM): "Mrs. Peiyi, we need to use your daughter's voice but her teeth are a little, how you say, snaggledy, so we're going to pretend the prettier kid's doing the singing, okeydokey?"

Mama Peiyi (MP): "Do whaaaaat???"

CPM: "Don't worry. It is still a great honor to you and your ancestors to have even a small part in this most magnificent ceremony ever staged in the history of the Olympics.

Now. Please tell your obviously genetically inferior daughter that it has been decided."

MP: "You want my daughter to sing but you want everybody else to think it's another kid that you think is cuter?"

CPM (relieved): "Ah, yes! That's it exactly. Of course, we will compensate you for this inconvenience (fumbling through tote bag). Yes! Here it is! An officially sanctioned souvenir bird's nest Olympic Stadium ashtray and cigarette lighter combo."

MP: "Are you trippin'? My kid doesn't smoke."

CPM: "Well, of course not. She's only seven. You should probably set it aside in a safe place until she's nine."

MP: "My daughter's earned the right to sing. She's rehearsed for weeks!"

CPM: "Oh, cry me a Yangtze. Your daughter's not the only one we've insulted. At first, we picked a ten-year-old but, ultimately, she just looked too old. You know how it is. You say ten-year-old and right away everybody's asking, 'Who's the hag?' Look, it's in the national interest that the child who sings 'Hymn to the Motherland' be flawless in appearance, and I believe it's obvious that your daughter could easily eat an egg roll through a picket fence. I mean no disrespect."

MP: "You looked in a mirror lately, asshole? You're uglier than a bucket of armpits."

CPM: "Madame! May I remind you that this is a very serious matter. Everything must be perfect. Perfect voice, perfect looks! Oh, why can't you embrace perfection like that nice American woman Kate Gosselin?"

MP: "You ain't perfect. In fact, you're a mo-ron. Anybody can look at you and tell the wheel's still a-turnin' but the hamster's dead."

CPM (happily distracted): "Mmmmm, hamster . . ."

Which is to say that a Southern woman defends her progeny ferociously and it's hard to imagine anything else. It's a statistical fact that a Southern mama is more likely to plunge a butter knife into the gut of anyone who would ever hurt her baby girl, even if that baby girl is old enough to wear faux denim Koret pantsuits and order "senior coffee." You don't ever read headlines about a mama in, say, North Dakota, plotting to kill off her daughter's competition for head cheerleader or prom queen. No, no. It's always some crazy-ass Southern mama being led away in handcuffs wearing sweatpants and a huge T-shirt that reads DANCE MOM! in glitter.

And a Southern mother of an only child (like me) is worst of all.

I'll give you an example. This week, the Princess has been at her first sleepaway camp. (And yes, I'm going to call it "sleepaway college" when she goes.) She'll swim, canoe, and learn to sail. I'll mope, pout, and be a little ashamed that I paid the extra ten bucks so the camp could e-mail me photos of her enjoying camp, updated hourly.

So while she thinks she's making papier-mâché crafts and learning how to use a bow and arrow and dive off a diving board into water that, frankly, doesn't look all that clean to me, away from the prying eyes of her meddlesome mommie, it's not exactly so.

The old hippie in me can't believe I've done this. Camp should be her personal retreat, not an excuse for me to spy. Shades of Big Brother.

But I can't help myself, and this is the lot of the mother of an only child.

I'm fairly certain that if the Gosselins sent their brood off to summer camp, they'd just toast their good fortune with wholesome glasses of sparkling cider and tell Aunt Jodi to drive them to the airport.

For me there's an heir, but no spare, and that's why I sat, one day into camp, clicking on the hourly photos and wondering who the hell this kid was who appeared to be sitting too close to Soph on the hayride and looked like a Jonas Brother.

I haven't decided whether or not to tell her I was spying but it'll probably spill out with something like: "Those cinnamon rolls at your breakfast Tuesday morning looked amazing. But why did you have to share half of yours with that Jonas wannabe. Was that a pencil-thin mustache?"

The last pictures of the day showed the Princess wearing someone else's clothes. Zoom in. Oh, it's her best friend's outfit.

One day in and she'd already used up five of the ten outfits I packed for her plus some of her friend's.

And she'd done something funky with her hair, too. Zoom in closer . . . enlarge photo . . . Oh. Never mind.

That's not her. Shit. I just clicked to buy a photo of some-body else's kid. I was officially nuts.

One thing was sure when I saw the end-of-day pictures. She hadn't applied nearly enough of the SPF 50 that I bought for her. There appeared to be too much pink on her shoulders and the tip of her nose. Ohmigod! There was a Band-Aid on her left knee. And it wasn't even a cute one. I wanted to weep.

Compare and contrast this with the Gosselins, who could easily miss one of their kids showing up at the dinner table with a severed limb.

Kate: "Jon, could you go outside and get Mady's arm?"

Jon (whining): "I dunno. Isn't it your turn? I got the last one."

OK, to be honest, burned and scarred as she is, the Princess seemed to be having the time of her life. Away from me. And this was as it should be. Although, thanks to the wonder of digital uploads, she was never as far away from me as she thought. Heh-heh-heh.

By the middle of the week, the guilt had set in and I resolved not to look at the photos for the rest of the week. Something about it just didn't feel right.

I let her daddy do it.

Here's the perfect way to lure kids out of the road and into the house, although I'm sure Kate Gosselin wouldn't approve of all the processed ingredients. Then again, who cares? Your kids will *love* this.

WICKED EASY CHOCOLATE KID PLEASER

1 (16-ounce) can chocolate syrup
¾ cup peanut butter
19 ice cream sandwiches
1 (12-ounce) container Cool Whip
1 cup salted peanuts

Pour chocolate syrup into a medium microwave-safe bowl and heat two minutes on high, making sure it doesn't boil. Stir peanut butter into hot chocolate until smooth. Let this cool until it's room temperature.

Line the bottom of a 9-X-13-inch baking dish with a layer of ice cream sandwiches. Spoon half the chocolate mixture on top; spoon half the Cool Whip on top of that, then half the peanuts. Repeat layers. Freeze until firm, about an hour. To serve, cut into squares. Makes about eighteen kid-sized servings, six grown-up servings.

12

Clay Aiken Ain't Marrying Your Glandular Daughter

Over the years, there have been a few unfortunate times when not everyone got the memo that I write a humor column.

Instead, the column is taken seriously, which can cause some very hard feelings and lots of angry "and-your-little-dog-too" type mail.

My standard reply to the more vitriolic mail used to be: "Dear Irritated Reader: I write a humor column in the same manner as that of the late Dave Barry's, except I get paid a lot less and I rarely write about boogers. Oh, and he's not really dead. I was just messin' wid ya."

I would never imply that these overreacting readers are humor-impaired. Rather, I believe they are stupid.

OK, that didn't come out right. I think they're, by and

large, very earnest but misguided folks who probably believed Barry when he wrote that aliens lived in his underpants.

"It must be so uncomfortable!" I imagine someone writing Barry. "Can you tell me: Does the alien look like Alf? I like spaghetti, do you?"

All of this is to say that sometimes it's the things you least expect that end up getting you in trouble with the haters. I'm recalling the great Angry Knitters United of two thousand ought five, who had an unexpectedly violent reaction to my, I thought, lighthearted lampoon of the proliferation of stitch-and-bitch clubs at coffeehouses. And by proliferation, I mean how there was a while there that you couldn't drink an overpriced vanilla latte without finding a couple of strands of mohair floating on top. Ah yes, there was a time when between the knitters and the nursing moms, there was scarcely any room for the poser writing bad poetry on his laptop at the local Starbucks. The common denominator of all three was really ugly footwear. I'm just saying.

But as whiny as the knitters were, they weren't nearly as mean as the nightmare-inducing rage of the restless leg syndrome sufferers who wanted to hobble me like Kathy Bates did to James Caan in *Misery*.

"I hope you get restless leg syndrome in spades one day," said one angry writer who was pissed that I thought it was hilarious that one of the drugs used to treat RLS lists "compulsive gambling" as a side effect.

Hmmm. Spades. Interesting word choice, no? The notion that casinos and gambling boats are full of zonked-out RLSers who wonder the next day why they have swizzle sticks in their pajama pockets is just too delicious.

Apparently the notion that I thought the *drug* was funny, not the ailment, was lost in translation.

The hate mail came from everywhere: I even heard from both people who live in Wyoming.

A reader in upstate New York was disappointed in my "lack of journalistic ethics." Yeah, me too. Whatever that is.

"I can't believe a responsible journalist would write such a demeaning editorial," wrote a Florida reader.

OK, so (a) I'm not a responsible journalist, so stop calling me names—I write pee jokes, for heaven's sake; and (b) I can't write editorials because that would require me to learn about important world issues, which would definitely eat into the time I have to do the stuff that really matters, like watching reruns of *Scott Baio Is 45 . . . And Single* on VH1.

The knitters and the RLSers were plenty pissed, but it was the Claymates who took hatin' to new heights—or lowts, as it were.

See, it's always the gentle references that backfire, the easy joke, the quick quip, if you will. The itsy, tiny four-word phrase implying that Clay Aiken wears women's clothing.

And so it was that I became the target of the Clay Aiken Defenders League Poutfest of 2008.

Most of them said I was implying he was gay and, long story short, how dare I?

Here's the thing: When a celebrity arranges to have a turkey-baster-style baby with a fifty-year-old woman "friend," all bets are off, hons. You're in the Big Leagues of Weird Celebritydom when that happens. Own it. Relish it. Bathe in its intoxicatingly skewed stew.

Here's a small sampling from the anthrax-soaked mail-bag:

"How can you sleep at night? I wish I believed in voodoo so I could procure an ugly doll that looks very much like you and find someone who would give you a wild ride issuing pain upon you. How did you get your job, anyway? With the assistance of your probation officer?"

OK, first off . . . procure? And secondly, leave my P.O. outta this.

Another got right to the point, sans threat of juju: "In case you haven't noticed, you are a jerk. I wish you huge failures in your career."

Well, no, I hadn't noticed that jerk thing, but then it's really hard for a jerk to recognize his or her own jerkdom. Donald Rumsfeld still has no clue, for example. So I guess I'll just have to take your word for it, person whom I've never met and who hasn't met me.

As for huge failures in my career, don't worry. I can hardly concentrate with these awful stabbing pains being issued all over my body.

"Can't you find a better way to make people laugh?" wrote

another. Well, sure. But going house-to-house with a whoopee cushion just seems so, I dunno, Arte Johnson retro.

"I wish you can't-get-a-job journalists could get a *real* job."

Well, this *is* my real job. Go frikkin' figure! Ouch! I think my eyeball just fell out.

This next one made me laugh so hard I turned inside out.

"Dear Ms. Rivenbark: I opened my newspaper this morning and was horrified to see you taking a potshot at a celebrity!"

Oh, no! How could I? Why, that would be like making fun of Paris Hilton or Lindsay Lohan or Kim Kardashian. Who would do such a horrible thing to our nation's most talented and deserving, uh, nation-spawn?

A potshot at a celebrity? You mean like the time I made fun of Matthew McConaughey for saying that his girlfriend "had a baby three months growing in her womb"? I mean, they shoulda just rounded up the *People* magazine editorial board and knocked on the door of that tricked-out toaster of a trailer home he lives in and demanded that he return his Sexiest Man Alive award for saying something so icky. And who wants to bet the baby mama gets tired of that whole living-in-a-trailer thing. "Fool," I imagine her saying, "my baby ain't crawling on plastic grass." Next she'll want an ottoman that isn't a cooler and lamps instead of paper lanterns. And because Matthew wants to get it right, he'll say "Aiiight, milady," because he'll know it's time to grow up, gnarly as it seems, and move the fam into a Brentwood mansion and settle for driving the house around on weekends.

Don't get me wrong, though. If I was stranded on a desert island and duh-hubby had sadly floated out to sea, I'd wish for nothing more than for Matthew to show up on his surfboard to rescue me. OK, well actually I'd rather see a delivery truck loaded with nothing but Lorna Doones, but it's an island and I'm trying to be realistic here.

Then there was this: "Clay Aiken has said time and time again that he is a heterosexual male," wrote one reader. "Why don't you take his word for it?"

Uh, yes, well. I believe the cat is out of the Hermès messenger bag on that one now and no one cares except perhaps a few thousand overwrought Claymates who feel strangely cheated.

I don't know how they didn't catch on but I do think Clay would've come out a lot sooner if these freaks weren't so middle-age swoony over him and, being a nice North Carolina boy, he hated to disappoint.

I repeat: Average heterosexual men don't father children by artificially inseminating women friends old enough to be their mamas. (See Jackson, comma Michael.)

Another writer said: "You're not stupid [Hey! A kind word at last!] but you are definitely a jerk [OK, never mind]. And, by the way, I was just watching a tribute to the late Tim Russert and you are no Tim Russert."

Well, no. At least we could agree on that much. Now, if

only I could get rid of these stabbing pains in my assular region.

And then there was this day-brightener: "You are a horrible person to bash such a positive Christian role model for our kids today as Mr. Clay Aiken. Shame on you! Please write me back so I can understand why you don't pick on the really negative actors, musicians, and politicians that are ruining our children today."

Oh, but I do! Where were you, letter writer, when I said that we needed Posh and Becks living in America almost as much as a supper of warm beer and tongue casserole. Thanks ever so, mother country. (Although, to be fair, big sloppy smooches for sending us *The Office*.)

I pick on plenty of doltish celebs, although I don't think they have the capacity to "ruin our children." I prefer to leave that to the parents themselves, instead of the funny-looking little people living inside the TV box.

To be fair, David Beckham, who seems like an amiable enough chap, didn't ruin our children but rather inspired an entire generation of polite young Indian girls to want to "bend it," whatever the hell that means. So, yes! I try to pick on others as often as possible and am more than a little hurt that you haven't even noticed.

One of my absolute favorite letters came from a woman who suggested that I do a little more research before I imply that Clay Aiken was anything less than an ice-road trucker.

"Do you even know that the people who work with him think he's courteous and kind to everyone? You might want to check with the employees at the Schubert Theater to find out what kind of a person he is."

For the record, I am sure that Clay Aiken is absolutely, hands-down the most macho person ever to play Sir Robin, the waifish tights-wearin' antihero in *Spamalot*. No question.

So Clay's come out now, bless God, and we can all get back to our lives. Well, not quite all of us.

Now some of his most devoted fans are turning on him for misleading them, lying to them and, hey, as it turns out, when he was singing all those love songs, it didn't necessarily mean that he was singing personally and privately to them *or* their woefully obese daughters. Hey, sorry if the truth hurts but I believe we've all established that I'm (a) not nice (b) not Tim Russert, and (C) on parole.

One former Claymate posted her final message on his fan site with this gem: "I will never be able to listen to him sing, 'O Holy Night,' knowing he desires unholy nights."

I imagine a certain voodoo priestess is out there somewhere sticking pins in a handmade doll with red-straw hair and an impish face, possibly from her prison cell. "You (stab!) said you'd (stab!) wait for me (stab!)."

What the Claymates didn't get was that I like Clay Aiken. I'm thrilled that he came out so his baby boy could be raised by a daddy living his authentic life instead of sneaking around the way poor, dead Rock Hudson (and so many more) had to do back in the day.

Face it, Clay Nation, this is progress. Now close your eyes and think of England when Clay sings. I promise he sounds just as good as he used to back when he was a heterosexual.

13

What? Your Preacher Doesn't Stand on a Bucket?

Growing up in a tiny town in rural southeastern North Carolina had its own brand of excitement.

For instance, I went to school side by side with royalty, sharing study hall with the reigning North Carolina pork queen, who even had a pig nose though, mercifully, it wasn't quite as obvious as Christina Ricci's in *Penelope*.

Duplin County, North Carolina, had miles of chicken houses, turkey farms, and hog "parlors," a funny word that always made me picture enormous pink-eyed sows lolling about on velvet-covered Duncan Phyfe sofas and watching their offspring tousling playfully on an Oriental rug.

Hogs seemed to invite euphemisms. Hog waste was disposed of in a "lagoon," which conjured up images of a young Brooke Shields and her tow-headed young lover cavorting in crystal waters. "Lagoon" sounded ever so much more exotic.

There were lots of hog lagoons in Duplin County because, at one time, we were the nation's number-one pork-producing county. I'll never forget the horror of discovering that a pond admired from a distance was in fact a hog lagoon. Sadly, this was confirmed only after we got the johnboat safely off its trailer and into the water. This was one of those embarrassing "sure is peaceful out here, can't believe nobody else has found this pond" kind of moments that turns into, "Oh, hell, this is a hog lagoon!", realizing that we wouldn't be catching any crappie that day but could perhaps catch plenty of crap. Oh, the shame of having to motor that little boat back out of the river of shit and onto the trailer and hope to God nobody saw us.

Rural counties in the South are full of characters, and we had more than our share in Duplin County, which was home of the world's largest frying pan in addition to the pig queen with the snout nose. The frying pan was so big that when the Lions Club fired it up with a bunch of tobacco barn burners, they used pitchforks to turn the whole chickens as they bubbled and browned.

If you got sick, you went to a doctor who thought that daylight savings time was from the devil and so you always knew to go one hour later for your appointment. Occasionally, a Yankee who had been transferred to Duplin County to work at the Butterball turkey plant would show up for his appointment at the time he was given, but other than that, everybody pretty much played by the rules.

For a time, we had a lot of tent revivals, and that's when

the true eccentrics crawled out of their falling-down ante-bellum homes and made their way to the tent pitched in the vacant lot beside the Branch Banking & Trust Building to stand and sway beside the trailer-home crowd.

One day, the Reverend Jim Whitting*ton* ("I pronounce it *ton* because my name carries a lot of weight with God!") came to call and drew quite a crowd because he, unlike most of the ragtag evangelists who passed through town in one shiny, sweat-soaked suit after another, was on channel nine every Sunday morning, screaming of salvation and healing and speaking in tongues.

One of the wealthier women in town showed up in her almost-new Jaguar to present the Reverend Whittington with a wad of cash to buy a prayer cloth, which he anointed on the spot by pressing the cloth to his huge lumpy forehead and going "hominahominahomina" over it. She watched him with such rapture, I'll never forget it, seeing a great healer in this slick creep whose knees sank softly into the tent's sawdust floor, one eye open to watch as crumpled fives and tens found their way into an aquarium at the makeshift altar where he prayed.

Proper church folks were, naturally, offended at the huge crowds these opportunistic leeches tended to draw. Me? I couldn't get enough of them. I've always been fascinated by religious freakiness.

The freakiest of all in our town was a middle-aged black woman with a lopsided wig who walked along the highway smack through the middle of town wearing at least four coats in the summertime and trailing an assortment of foster children behind her, each more pitiful than the one before. "Sister Admira" was crazier'n a sprayed roach. On odd days, she'd position herself in front of the Ben Franklin to scream "words what have come to me straight from the Almighty Jehovah himself" from the top of an overturned scrub bucket. Usually it boiled down to how we were all going to hell. After a few months of this, some asshole gave her a megaphone and she didn't mind using it.

"Sin brought 'em into this world," she'd shriek into the megaphone, her wig jerking from its sideways perch like it had a rat running around underneath, as she pointed at her sad-eyed charges one by one. "And only God can take 'em out!"

Fortunately, Child Protective Services took 'em all out after some kind Christian finally reported that Sister Admira's young charges were traipsing around behind her all week long instead of going to school. She eventually went to the "crazy hospital" an hour away where someone said she was still preaching from the top of a scrub bucket, her new congregation calmly ignoring her while they watched *Good Times* on the overhead TV.

It occurred to me only a little while ago that people who don't grow up in small towns might not have close encounters of the kind we had with Sister Admira.

With Sister gone to the nuthouse and a general feeling that it was a bad idea to allow any more TV preachers into town to fleece the locals, all we had left besides mainstream Baptist, Methodist, and Presbyterian churches was a sweet-faced woman who called herself reverend and decorated cakes at the Piggly Wiggly for free.

Although Reverend Brenda had never technically had any formal religious or cake-decorating training, she was filled with the spirit and chose to share it, not from a scrub bucket rimmed by a half-dozen shoeless retarded children, but by witnessing through cake and coffee.

Reverend Brenda was available at a moment's notice to "cast out demons" or to create a masterpiece in buttercream fondant for your bridal shower. If these two needs converged, well that was all the better.

My first personal encounter with Reverend Brenda came when I went to pick up my friend Darinda to go to the football game at Legion Stadium one cold October night and discovered that Darinda's mama had called over Reverend Brenda to cast out an alcoholic demon from her husband.

"Daddy's drinkin' again," Darinda whispered to me as she fumbled into her navy peacoat. "Mama says that only God and Reverend Brenda can help him now."

I knew from gossip that Reverend Brenda was a frequent visitor at the hospital twenty miles away and had even managed to bribe a "clergy" parking sticker from one of the ward clerks so she could park right beside the doctors and other important people. She considered it her Christian duty to check on the lost sheep at the hospital, although usually the rooms were crowded enough.

In the South, families set siege when a relative is hospitalized. My friend Pam says she can turn hospital chairs into a bed, locate the extra linens, find the ice, and memorize the daily cafeteria specials in under five minutes. Reverend Brenda could do all of that *and* transform a cooler into an ottoman/kneeling bench.

"Looks like it was an emergency visit," I said, noting that Reverend Brenda was pressing both her hands on the top of Darinda's daddy's head and moaning something suspiciously close to "hominahominahomina."

"Yeah, you noticed, huh?"

It was hard to miss the fact that Darinda's daddy was sitting bolt upright in his scratchy plaid recliner wearing nothing but his huge, puffy white boxer shorts. He was an exceedingly large man covered with moles and it is a sight that I won't forget as long as I live—Reverend Brenda's hands, green icing still under the nails from a Halloween party cake, pressed to Darinda's daddy's temples while he leaned forward like he was getting a pressure check at the eye doctor.

I had the feeling that Darinda's mama had given her husband an "old tomato": Either let Reverend Brenda lay healing hands on his fevered alcoholic brain or she'd be leaving him and taking Darinda and her little brother with her.

Reverend Brenda didn't seem to mind that we had intruded on her healing and demon-casting-out service. As we got ready to leave, she even broke away from her tongue-speaking long enough to cheerily tell us that we both looked "cuter'n a sack full of puppies," adding, "y'all girls have fun at the ball game and don't fornicate under the bleachers 'cause you know a man won't marry a woman with the dirty leg."

"Didn't plan on it," I said under my breath while being vaguely creeped out at the notion of the "dirty leg." I was almost positive that phrase was nowhere to be found in the King James version of the Bible.

"We might smoke some weed, though," said Darinda, mostly under her breath.

We giggled at this and ran out the door, hoping that Reverend Brenda hadn't heard that last part. She meant well and there was no denying that she was good at her day job, having once created an astonishingly lifelike spun-sugar rendering of the faces of Abraham Lincoln, Martin Luther King Jr., and John F. Kennedy Jr. on a vanilla sheet cake for the ribbon-cutting ceremonies at the new town hall.

She also made a red velvet cake that you'd crawl over twenty miles of broken glass to have the chance to eat. And she was the most cheerful somebody I'd ever met. If you asked Reverend Brenda how she was doing, she'd always smile real big and say, "Honey, if my life gets any better, I'm gonna have to hire somebody to help me enjoy it."

Reverend Brenda's red velvet cake was created as a godly alternative to devil's food cake, which she refused to make or decorate for obvious reasons. Ditto her feelings about partaking of that famous Southern Christmas delicacy: divinity fudge.

"There's nothing Christlike about fudge," she'd say, refusing to eat it even under the more politically correct name that even the holinesses who didn't shave their legs and lived on the dirt roads would use: seafoam candy.

In the rural South, even food had the capacity to offend the Almighty. Some folks I knew wouldn't eat deviled eggs because of the name, which made them almost but not quite as crazy as Sister Admira in my mind.

I've never met a deviled egg I didn't love. They're a pure pleasure and you can dress them up as much or as little as you like. Here's one of my favorite variations.

HEAVENLY DEVILED EGGS

1 dozen hard-cooked eggs
6 tablespoons mayonnaise (yes, Duke's again)
2 teaspoons prepared horseradish
2 tablespoons sweet pickle juice
1 teaspoon black pepper
¼ teaspoon salt

Split the eggs lengthwise; remove yolks and mash 'em up with the mayo, horseradish, pickle juice, pepper, and salt. If you want to get fancy, you can blend this together in a food processor 'til creamy, pour it into a cake-decorator bag (or a Ziploc bag with one corner cut) and pipe the filling into the egg-white halves. Garnish with paprika 'cause it just looks more festive.

CLASSIC RED VELVET CAKE

In the South, we love our artificial red food coloring and we're not ashamed to admit it. You won't care about the health and safety of it once you taste this Southern classic, which is always welcome at wakes and weddings alike.

2½ cups flour
½ cup cocoa powder
1 teaspoon baking soda
½ teaspoon salt
2 sticks butter, softened
2 cups sugar
4 eggs
8 ounces sour cream
½ cup milk
1 (1-ounce) bottle red food coloring
2 teaspoons vanilla extract
Cream cheese frosting (recipe follows)

Sift flour, cocoa powder, baking soda, and salt; set aside. Beat butter and sugar in large bowl with electric mixer for 6 minutes or until fluffy-looking. Add eggs in, one at a time. Add sour cream, milk, red food coloring, and vanilla. Gradually beat in the flour mixture until blended. If you overdo it, your cake won't be as moist and soft, so just don't.

Pour batter into two greased and floured 9-inch

cake pans and bake for about 35 minutes at 350 degrees. (Use a cake tester to make sure it's done.) Cool the layers on a wire rack and frost with classic cream cheese frosting made by mixing together these ingredients 'til fluffy:

8 ounces cream cheese, softened
½ stick butter, softened
2 teaspoons vanilla extract
4 cups confectioner's sugar

This recipe makes enough to frost one fabulous cake. When you get really expert at red velvet cake, you might want to try your hand at making one in the shape of an armadillo like they did for the groom's cake in *Steel Magnolias*.

14

Chances of Getting in the Hall of Fame? Very Rare

Duh-hubby looked at me with loving eyes as he gently held out my coat and waited for me to slip into it.

"What's up?"

"I'm taking you to the Outback," he said.

While more monied folks might think this meant that he was spontaneously whisking his bride of nearly twenty years away on an Australian adventure, I knew better.

We are attentive Kmart shoppers, after all. People in our income bracket don't just jump on a plane and fly eighteen hours on a romantic whim. He meant the Outback Steakhouse, which was fine with me. I'm a big enough redneck to believe that going to Epcot is almost as good as crossing the pond. It-lee and a whole bunch of other countries and you never even have to leave Orlando! Suh-weet!

The truth was, I knew why Duh had selected Outback, but he felt the need to explain anyway.

"The winner of the Duplin County Hall of Fame always gets the award at a fancy steak dinner," he said. Did his voice just catch a bit? He cleared his throat and continued.

"And, although they didn't pick you again this year, I just want you to know that you'll always be in *my* hall of fame."

"Honey, that's real sweet," I said. And it was. It was almost enough to make me forgive him for nominating me for ten years in a row in the first place.

"Ridiculous!" I had huffed a decade ago. "Why, there are many more deserving natives than I. This will just be embarrassing!"

Even as I was saying it, though, I figured I might have a smallish shot at it. But that last flicker of hope had been snuffed out seven years earlier when I heard a rumor that they might give the award to a native whose "fame" had apparently included working on a movie one time as a stand-in for Henry Winkler.

"Heeeeeyyyyy."

I knew that the trip to Outback was because the rejection letter had arrived the day before. For the tenth year in a row, I wasn't a winner. Which made me a loser. Again.

Since y'all know a little about my home county now, perhaps you should also know that the population is so small that they're going to run out of people and have to start giving the award to farm animals. So, at this rate, I stand a fairly good chance of losing out to a chicken. And if that happens, somebody's gonna die. I'm not kidding.

The rejection letter always says the same thing: "All nominees are deserving of the honor and recognition of receiving the award, for they have contributed in a significant manner to the growth, development, and well-being of Duplin County, North Carolina, the United States, and/or the world and its people."

OK, maybe I'm not deserving of being considered. After all, I can't honestly say that writing a few books and a humor column that runs in a few newspapers has exactly helped the well-being of "the world and its people."

After ten years of rejection, I'm feeling like a younger, fatter Susan Lucci, although even she eventually got her Daytime Emmy.

Because there are actually two Hall of Fame recipients announced each year—one living and one deceased—I'm starting to wonder if I'm going to have to die to win this thing. I've got my pride, hons. If they pick me posthumously, I won't show up to accept it or to enjoy the much ballyhooed "nice steak dinner."

Which brings us back to Outback, where Duh had invited his redneck cousin, Dink, to join us. And, yes, it says "Dink" on his birth certificate. This is the South; pay attention.

The waitress greeted us and shot me a look that seemed to convey pity. How could she know my secret shame? Did I have "loser" written all over me? I considered resubmitting my own application to the Hall of Fame and mentioning that I had once had an entire conversation with the girl who plays Peyton on *One Tree Hill* when they filmed across the street from my house. Fonzie that.

We settled ourselves into the booth beneath the slightly creepy gaze of a stuffed koala bear clinging to a plastic replica of a eucalyptus tree. Travel broadens the mind so.

Dink was in town for a convention of fellow fastener salespeople. He started to tell me more about that but I fell face forward into my kookaburra cocktail from the sheer drudgery of it.

Kidding! Dink can make any story livelier. He's a classic Bubba, the kind who not only helps you tote off the oyster shells after the roast but drops them into a neighbor's driveway to fill in a pothole he noticed.

Dink was telling an extremely funny joke about how a group of kindergarteners were being told not to use baby talk anymore.

"The teacher says to 'em, 'From now on, you just use big-people words.' Then she says to 'em, 'Now tell me what y'all did this weekend'," drawls Dink.

"So when one little boy says he went to visit his nana the teacher says, 'You mean your grandmother.' Then another boy says he rode a choo-choo and the teacher says, 'You mean you rode the train.' Then a third little boy says he read a book and the teacher smiles and asks, 'What book did you read?' and the little boy thinks for a minute, then puffs his chest out really big, all proud of his answer, and says, 'Winnie the *Shit!*'"

Well, what can I tell you? I forgot all about my Hall of Fame diss and couldn't stop laughing.

Sometimes a night out with your super red cousin-in-law is just what the doctor ordered.

It was time to order so I told the waitress I'd like my favorite: the eight-ounce Victoria's filet, cooked medium.

The waitress looked at me and said, "Medium. Now that's done on the outside with a warm, pink center, OK?"

I thought this was a little weird but, hell, maybe she just had a slight hearing problem and wanted to make sure she had it right.

"Yes," I said. "Fortunately, our understanding of 'medium' is exactly the same." I hated the snarkiness in my voice, but the kookaburra cocktail and Dink's joke had me feeling a little bitchy/silly.

She then turned to Duh, who ordered his Outback special, a twelve-ounce sirloin, medium rare.

"Hmmmm," said the waitress. "That's going to be pink inside fading to a grayish brown color throughout the rest of the meat and with a grayish-brown outside."

"Yes!" said hubby as if he'd just proved to be more intelligent than a fifth grader. I was afraid he was going to pump his fist in the air.

Meantime, all that talk about gray meat was making me a

little sick. Or maybe it was the bloomin' onion, which Dink ordered for the table but which I had demolished in my Hall of Fameless–induced depression.

The waitress turned to Dink, who also ordered the Outback special, but cooked rare.

Once again, the waitress took on a look of concentration like she was going to kinetically cook it by using her own thought rays.

"Rare . . . That's—"

But Dink held up his hand to stop her. Uh-oh. I knew what was coming.

"I dunno about all that, lil darlin'," he drawled. "Just knock his ears off, wipe his ass, and lead 'im to the table."

The waitress looked down at the descriptions that Outback had provided and pondered, I thought, the proper response. It was obvious to me that Outback was sick and damn tired of dealing with idiots who send their steaks back whining about degrees of doneness. There are just some things in this life that we should all agree on without a lot of explanation, including the definitions of rare, medium rare, medium, and (shudder) well done, which is also defined as "charred on the outside without a remnant of juiciness left intact."

Dink laughed at his own joke and the waitress looked mildly uncomfortable. Clearly she wasn't used to being in the company of a high-dollar fastener salesman.

"Right," she said. "Rare."

"I mean reaaaal rare, baby girl. Listen here. When you

bring that steak out I wanna be able to tell you that I've seen cows get well that weren't hurt any worse than that."

Then he rocked back in his chair and laughed at his own cleverness all over again.

"OK," said the waitress—gamely, I thought.

"You owe her a big tip," I hissed at Dink after she'd finally left, presumably to bring us water, which would probably be cold, induced by its proximity to ice.

His dopey LIFE IS GOOD T-shirt stretched tight over his enormous belly, Dink picked at the greasy remnants of the bloomin' onion and seemed content to picture his Outback special mooing noisily on the grill for a few fleeting seconds before being led to its plate.

He started telling about how his friend in South Carolina had "kilt" a five-and-a-half-foot-long timber rattlesnake, soaked it overnight in milk, dipped it in batter, and fried it 'til it was crispy. Being health conscious, they served it with salads. Dink said his friend kept the snake alive in a barrel overnight until his grandson could come see it the next day and feed the rattles to his pet ants. Did Dink know anybody normal? I mean, besides us?

Meanwhile, my thoughts wandered to the steak dinner I wasn't going to be having at the Hall of Fame banquet that night.

At this rate, they'd go to the crazy house and give the damn award to that crazy-ass Sister Admira before I'd ever get it. She could bring along her bucket and stand on it to make her acceptance speech.

In the meantime, all I could do would be to watch the mailbox every October, sulk a bit and, oh yes, one more thing, continue to work on my newest book: *Duplin County: Gateway to Paradise!*

That oughta learn 'em.

Dink, who is usually about as sensitive as a toilet seat, noticed that I wasn't as cheerful as usual, despite having just eaten most of a bloomin' onion and a perfectly medium Victoria's filet.

Finally, after a (very) little amount of prodding, I told him about the whole Hall of Fame shame thing.

He shook his big curly head in sympathy. Like any good Bubba, he stands ready to defend the honor of a Southern woman who has been forced, through no fault of her own, to endure some trauma or other.

After listening to me and wiping the last bit of cow blood off his stubble, Dink leaned forward and said that I should always remember the words of his granddaddy who had raised him.

I braced myself for something wise and useful. Dink, like most Bubbas, could be quite insightful and kind when you least expected it.

"Always remember one thing in this life," he said, pausing to stare at the koala's big brown glass eyes. I knew he woulda shot it if we were really in the wild.

"What is it, Dink? What should I remember? I could really use some perspective here."

"Always remember . . . you can't drink all day if you don't start in the mornin'."

And with that pronouncement, Dink laughed loud enough to make the boomerang nailed to the wall above our booth rattle a bit.

True that, I thought.

Dink, Duh, and I are crazy about a good steak and even crazier about my almost-famous perfect prime rib with horsey sauce. It's supereasy but most people think it's a really big deal to make. I served this to friends for dinner one night when we rented an oceanfront cottage at Bald Head Island, a one-hour drive and twenty-minute ferry ride from my house. Bald Head doesn't allow any cars, so you ride around in little golf carts all day, exploring the island's maritime forest and beaches. At sunset, there's nothing like sipping cocktails on the porch of your cottage, listening only to gulls and the distant purring of golf carts while the amazing scent of this fragrant roast floats onto the deck and away on the ocean breeze. This recipe will always be in my culinary hall of fame, and it should be in yours, too.

EVERYONE'S-A-WINNER PRIME RIB

1½ teaspoons kosher salt
1 teaspoon pepper
1 tablespoon olive oil
6-pound prime rib roast (3 ribs)

Combine salt, pepper, and oil and rub evenly over roast. Place roast on wire rack in a foil-lined roasting pan. Bake at 450 degrees for 45 minutes; reduce heat to 350 degrees and bake 45 minutes longer (or until meat thermometer reads 145 degrees). Remove from oven; cover loosely with foil. Let stand 20 minutes before carving. Serve with horseradish sauce made by combining 3 tablespoons prepared horseradish with 1/4 cup sour cream, a tablespoon of mayonnaise, and a teaspoon of Dijon mustard. Supereasy and super-good.

15

When Celia Met Sally...
A Convertible Love Story

There are two kinds of people in this world: those who drive convertibles and, well, the rest of y'all.

That's right, hons. Thanks to a whopping birthday surprise from duh-hubby, I have finally shed the abysmal anonymity that comes with driving a Ford Taurus. A tan Ford Taurus. A tan 1999 Ford Taurus, to be precise.

I believe I've made my point.

The delivery was successful, and it's a girl. At least that's what I like to think. She's red and shiny and, best of all, she's a Mustang with many horses under her hood and I love her more than cheese and TiVo *combined*.

The thing about "Sally" is that she is, unlike my tan Taurus, easy to locate in a parking lot.

Never again will I have to ask the security guard at the mall to ride me around in his little electric car like some kind of moron, trying to find my car. Who knew it was Na-tional Take Your Tan Taurus to the Mall Day?

I'll never forget the hopelessness in his voice when I de-scribed my car to the security guard.

"This may take a while," he said.

"Oh!" I said, suddenly cheerful. "I just remembered! *My* Taurus has a bumper sticker that says "I heart my cat."

"They all do," he replied, looking even sadder.

Now that I've got Sally, I understand how Harley owners feel. I've heard there's a secret Harley wave they've worked out so that even if they're driving a (snicker) Prius, they give the wave of brotherhood to a passing biker who then knows there's something infinitely more cool at home in the garage and that the (OK, now I'm laughing out loud) Prius is just being driven because the biker is on his way to take his ailing mama to the orthopedic doctor.

Convertible people, of which I am now one, did I men-tion, have a similar kinship on the road. Nothing is more embarrassing than to be caught top up on a warm, cloudless fall day, passed by another convertible with the top down, whose driver gives you a well-deserved, "man, what is your *problem?*" look.

I've actually pulled up beside another convertible, our tops down, my hair in a kerchief that is less Jackie O and more Lucy-stompin'-grapes and exchanged the knowing, self-satisfied smile of the Chosen.

Sometimes, sad to say, there is snobbery among the Cho-sen. For instance, I see how the guy with the BMW convertible looks at me as he takes his position in the carpool lane beside me at my kid's school. It is not an exaggeration to say that we rev our engines a little as we sit side by side.

He's pretending to ignore me but I know that's impossible. Mostly because it's hard to ignore the overwhelmingly cool sight of me singing "Cheeseburger in Paradise" into my hairbrush, with the top down, natch.

He's listening to his XM radio or something talky and pretending not to notice that Sally has a phenomenal stereo system.

"I like mine with lettuce and tomato! Heinz fifty-seven and french-fried potato! . . ."

Despite this impressive show, BMW dad is smug because, no doubt, his convertible was a lot more expensive than Sally. But Sally has heart, she's a real slice of Americana, something special, her shapely fortieth-anniversary edition lines reminding us of that sixties generation poised on the verge of rebellion. She is cool with a capital "Brrrrr."

The BMW convertible, on the other hand, is usually driven by men who work in vague and boring fields like finance and know nothing of blasting old Stones or Cream because that would interfere with their prolonged Bluetooth conversations with others of their own kind.

The only sour note since Sally came into my formerly beige life has been the inability of young men to mask their deep disappointment when they move closer to see the blonde in the hot red convertible only to discover that she is, well, their mother. They might want to work on that.

When they see me at the wheel, their faces drop in much the same way my daughter's does when she goes trick-or-treating with her friends and the asshole family hands out pencils.

But just because I'm nobody's version of a MILF or even a GMILF, it doesn't mean I am ready for the old folks' home. Women aren't aging like they used to; we're talking tough and driving fast cars. It's not easy being impossibly cool at my age, hons. The other day my daughter wanted to hide under Sally's floor mats when I announced, with radio blaring, that I really liked the artistic rap stylings of Florida.

"Did you just say Florida, like the state?" Soph asked.

"Well, sure, honey. It's f-l-o-r-i-d-a, right?"

"It's pronounced Flow-*ride*-uh," she said, barely able to control her contempt.

Oh.

"You didn't say that in front of anybody else, did you?" she asked, squinting at me through hands covering her face. She had the very same look I once gave my parents many years ago when they asked, "How'd he do?" after I came home from a Steely Dan concert. He???!!!!

"Of course I didn't say it in front of anyone else. For Christ's sake, I drive a convertible. I'm the *cool mommie!*"

"Florida!"

"Stop saying that!"

"Florida! Florida! Florida!"

"Grounded! Grounded! Grounded!"

Am I in some sort of second teenhood, driving a cool car and playing my music too loud?

We're all in some sort of acting-out crisis, it seems. I'll never forget Aunt Sudavee's horror when, just as she was preparing to take the first bite of her raisin toast with Promise spread, she heard Diane Keaton drop the F-bomb live and in person on *Good Morning America*.

Keaton's always been quirky and ageless, wearing her ubiquitous white suits and wattle-disguising scarves. Midway through a fluffy little plug for her latest movie, she got caught up in some sort of faux lesbian girl-crush rant about the beauty of Diane Sawyer's lips. As in, "If I had lips like that, I wouldn't have had to work on my f'ing personality."

"Well, I never!" Aunt Sudavee said, dropping her toast on the floor, Promise-side down, of course, 'cause that's just what kind of day it was going to be.

A couple of weeks later, just when Aunt Sudavee thought it was safe to return to morning TV, there was Jane Fonda dropping a bomb of her own during an interview with Meredith Vieira.

What did she say? Let's just say that I'm too much of a lady to speak or write it, so I'll just describe it as the big scary worst one that women never use, you know the one, it rhymes with *hunt*.

Unlike Sawyer, who giggled, licked her f'ing gorgeous lips provocatively and then threatened to wash Keaton's mouth out with soap, things didn't go so well at the *Today* show. Vieira returned from a hasty commercial break with a stiffly worded apology that just made things worse. I had the feeling that she thought Jane Fonda was a pretty big rhymes-with-hunt herself.

Fonda shouldn't have said it, but she was just quoting from her role in *The Vagina Monologues*, so there was some context to it.

Then, not a week later, there's that woozy old cougar, Kathleen Turner, dropping, not the effenheimer, but "ass-hole" during a live interview on local TV.

What's next? Roma Downey greeting the ladies of *The View* with "Whassup, bitches?"

Truthfully, I'd rather hear the rough talk than that weird Oprah baby talk.

Can we please sign a petition or something to get her to stop calling vaginas "vah-jay-jays."

Every time she says it, it's as if she's saying it for the first time, hooting and clapping her hands at her own cleverness.

What is she, two?

What's next? Telling us that she has trouble finding blouses that fit because of her enormous ninnie pies?

So what's with the aging movie-star potty-mouth syndrome? Maybe they're tired of the twits on *America's Next Top Model* having all the fun.

People always say that one of the perks of getting older is that you can get away with some major shit, which I guess is why Queen Elizabeth and Barbara Bush can hardly open their mouths without resorting to F-bombs. What? You never noticed that?

After a while, there will be a cussing revolution in the nursing homes with all these foul-mouthed old broads. The only good thing about being in the home is that people automatically assume you're at least a little bit crazy.

It's the same as how Gary Busey can get away with anything because he lost half his brains on the pavement in a motorcycle crash a few years back. So when he was shown licking Jennifer Garner at the Oscars like she was a toaster strudel, everybody just said, "That? Oh, that's just Gary."

If Gary had been driving a convertible instead of a motorcycle that fateful day, he'd still have his right mind.

Rage on, middle-age dames. Buy a convertible, keep the top down, and sing into your hairbrush all the way to flow-*ride*-uh.

16

I Want to be a Margo, but I'm Really a Sha-nae-nae

If you've been shopping for fashionable ladies' clothing lately (not you, Ryan Seacrest!), you may have noticed a weird naming trend embraced by mall fixtures like Ann Taylor, Banana Republic, and Coldwater Creek.

For instance, are you an "Audrey"? At Ann Taylor, that's the name of the pants that sits exactly on your natural waist, attends PTA meetings in a punctual manner, and always volunteers to help make the Popsicle-stick arks at vacation bible school. Audrey is the good girl, while "Margo," with a slightly dropped waist, is more of a loose cannon. Margo votes Democratic and once painted her dining room walls whorehouse-red "just because." A few racks over, "Lindsay" sits lowest of all on the waist. It's easy to imagine Audrey hanging on the rack and sniping that Lindsay really should act her age, not prance about looking like a sixteen-year-old sucking on frozen lemonade at Forever 21 where all of the clothes are probably named "Paris."

Over at Coldwater Creek, you can choose from the über-natural sounding "Willow," "Brook," and "Holly" clothing lines. The clothes don't look particularly outdoorsy, so the names are puzzling, but they're not nearly as curiously named as the ones at Banana Republic: "Martin," "Jackson," and "Harrison." I don't know where they get the idea that women want to buy clothes named after dead presidents, but then I'm not a marketing genius. Which may explain why my sausage-flavored frosting never took off.

I can't wait to see if this naming trend sifts down-market, as they say, to Walmart or Kmart, where things might get a little more real.

Frankly, "Margo" doesn't tell me anything. A pair of jeans named "Reba Fay" or "Sha-nae-nae" tells me right away that they're gonna fit perfectly—big in the ass and "relaxed in the thigh." Truth is, if my thighs get any more "relaxed," they're going to demand their own ticket to the Bahamas.

I've been sad to see the revival of "mom jeans," those disasters in denim with the nine-inch zippers and waistlines that threaten to crawl all the way up to your armpits.

They're hideous and nobody looks good in 'em, so they're not worth naming. But if they were, think "Ethel."

Mom jeans are the perfect storm of bad design: they broaden hips, flatten the butt, and taper in a ghastly fashion at the ankle. Extreme mom jeans even come in odious pale blue washes and feature an elastic waist that tells the world:

"Why, as a matter of fact, my idea of a good time *is* dinner at the Cracker Barrel at four P.M. followed by a *Murder, She Wrote* marathon on TNT."

The phrase "mom jeans" is so universally understood, it's even in the urban dictionary, which notes that they are "usually accompanied by a sexy cardigan boasting birds or wildlife and accented by a quilted purse."

Face it—when you're wearing hand-knit sparrows on your chest and mom jeans, the message is clear: You have officially stopped trying.

I was surprised when celebs started wearing "Ethel."

Fergie, she of the lovely lady humps, led the charge, followed by Mischa ("Feed me!") Barton, Scarlett Johansson, and even Jennifer Lopez who, I'm sure, is terribly upset that she couldn't find any that were trimmed in dead baby seal fur.

Of course, there are some women who are thrilled to have mom jeans back on the scene after years of too many lowrisers that celebrate, rather than reign in, the aptly named "muffin top," that unfortunate puff of belly fat. Maybe even the mom jean is better than super low-rise jeans that show the thong or the top two-thirds of an American Eagle flapping above the butt cheeks. It would be majestic, except it's not.

Ethel jeans will never be sexy. Even Jessica Simpson, photographed in her mom jeans, looked as if she needed to be hauling webbed chairs and Capri Suns out to the soccer fields instead of nibbling on Tony Romo's earlobe like it's a piece of cheese.

It would be easier if they named jeans for celebrities so you'd know exactly what you were getting without even having to try them on. "Mary-Kate" for itty-bitty jeans that come with a cartoonishly oversized caramel latte cup; "Angelina Jolie" for jeans that are sold with two tiny Cambodian orphans stitched right into the back pockets; "Katie Holmes," jeans which spell out "help me!" in the fabric if you look very closely; and "Dina Lohan," self-promoting stage mom of Lindsay, for jeans that look OK from a distance but, when you get closer, are actually completely transparent.

For men, there could be "David Hasselhoff" jeans, made entirely of cheese, and "John Mayer" jeans which, when removed, become instantly bored and walk themselves over to the house of the next "it" girl in Hollywood.

Victoria's Secret, once famous for its sweet-sounding "Emma" line, seems to be going in a different direction with its new ipex wireless bra, which doesn't scream sexy romance so much as it makes you remember it's time to pay your cell phone bill.

Something tells me Audrey would approve of this bra.

And speaking of buying a bra, why does this have to be such an ordeal?

People are constantly telling us that 80 percent of American women are wearing the wrong bra size. What? Do we just pick up somebody else's left behind in the dressing room? How can this be?

To answer the wretched revelation that many of us are walking around with droopy straps and back-fat spillage, most department stores are now employing "certified bra counselors" who have gone to actual classes for this.

The cool part is that they don't charge for this service. My friend Amy, who is always looking for a bargain, went for a fitting at one of the big department stores in the mall recently and reported that "the entire experience was perfect."

The certified bra fitter measured her up, down, and all around, taking about thirty minutes to pronounce the perfect size.

"I felt like we really bonded," said Amy. "I felt like I should've smoked a cigarette or had a glass of wine after it was over."

One of the reasons that the right bra size is so important is that researchers (boy ones, I'm guessing) have discovered that the wrong bra size can make women short-tempered.

This comes under the time-honored "no shit, Sherlock" school of statistical analysis.

Men are always trying to find out why a woman might be in a bad mood. Turns out, it's not because hubby hasn't helped out around the house since the Reagan administration. It's because our bras don't fit properly. Our collective bad.

Discover magazine, no less, reported that the right bra size is crucial to staying in a good mood because, if you wear a D cup in which both breasts have a combined weight of fifteen to twenty-three pounds, it could be "the equivalent of walking around all day carrying two small turkeys."

It's a powerful image, to be sure, but why stop there?

Why not four roasting hens, eight pork tenderloins, or sixteen bags of frozen chicken nuggets?

Still, it was hard to argue with Amy's delight at her brafitting experience. Appearance is very important to Amy, a definite "Lindsay" who keeps herself in tip-top shape through a regimen of vitamins, yoga, and other things that make me sleepy to think about.

Joining her one day at her country-club pool, she motioned to me to scoot toward her a bit on my chaise lounge.

"Honey," she said, reaching out to pat my hand, "you gotta work on your a-ree."

"My what?"

"Your a-ree, hon," she said, now whispering this weird word I'd never heard of.

Amy is the only person on God's green earth who can make me feel like I'm from Staten Island. She is purely, deeply Southern and, on top of that, she's *mountain* Southern, which has its own lexicon.

Apparently my "a-ree" was in the general vicinity of my naughties.

"Ohhhhh," I said, as Amy delicately removed her designer sunglasses and jutted her head forward like a chicken toward my fun box.

"This is my a-ree?" I asked, innocently.

"Sugar, of course. And you have to tend it better than, well, *that*."

She waved her hand in a dismissive circle and I realized that this was exactly the same scene played out in the *Sex and the City* movie between a perfectly groomed Samantha and the too-busy-to-care Miranda.

Amy continued, "You need special a-ree scissors that you only use for trimming and you need a clamshell mir-rie that fits in your palm just so and you need a special comb to collect all the, uh, trimmage."

Trimmage? Is that even a real word?

"Darlin,' I know that you've been busy what with your book tours and your fancy life but you simply can't ignore you're a-ree like that."

"Are you saying 'area'?"

"That's what I said—a-ree."

"You mean my, er, *bush?*"

At this word, Amy looked deeply insulted, although it was hard for me to see how "a-ree" was much better.

"Well now," she drawled in her aristocratic way, "That's just *common.*"

In the South, there is nothing worse than being "common." It's far worse than being "tacky," which is used by everyone. To be "common" is to have committed the vilest of lowlife offenses.

It is akin to another ultimate aristocratic Southern putdown used when confronted with the misbehavior of someone, be it the server at the club who has skimped on the amount of gin in the glass or the revelation that a beloved business partner has fled the country after embezzling from the company: "He (or she) just makes me taaaaarrrrdd." As in tired.

This whole discussion was making me taaarrrrdd, as Amy proceeded to tell me about the heirloom clamshell "mir-rie" her sainted grandmother had bequeathed her in her will for just such "a-ree maintenance."

I would've hoped more for the sterling silver iced-tea spoons myself, but sure, I guess the "trimmage" scissors and heirloom mirror are almost as good.

I placed the large towel that a nice young man handed me when I signed in (ohmigod, did the cabana boy notice my lack of a-ree upkeep?!) over my bottom half and told Amy about a wonderful new product I'd just heard about called Subtle Butt.

They're disposable gas neutralizing pads that you place inside your underwear so you can toot away and no one ever smells it. Not even he who dealt it.

"Heavenly Lord!" Amy said. "Who would use such a thing?"

"Well," I said, suddenly ashamed I'd even brought up Subtle Butt pads, "like if you're in a meeting and you really need to—"

"No!"

I looked around and realized that this was probably the very first time at this particular Southern country club that anyone had discussed activated carbon pads that let you poot in your underpants. Amy looked as if she was ready for me to go.

"But I haven't even gone in the pool yet!"

She lowered her sunglasses once again and looked in the direction of my neglected pum-pum.

"What? It's not like I'm gonna clog the pool drain."

"Of course not, darlin'. That would be . . . *common*."

I'd heard enough and decided to go. Frankly, it's hard to be at the pool with a hair-free "Lindsay" when you're rockin' the one-piece "Mamie" with the built-in "Slimsational" panel.

17

It Is What
It @#$%^-ing Is

Hons, it's a sad day when a woman can't cuss out her own toilet when it overflows.

"I was in my own house," said Dawn Herb of Scranton, Pennsylvania, after being charged with disorderly conduct for cussing. "It wasn't like I was outside or drunk."

Which, in the South, can often be redundant, depending on the neighborhood.

Chalk it up to one more difference between North and South that poor Dawn Herb was threatened with thirty days in jail (where the toilets don't even have lids!) just for screaming at her daughter to bring the @#$%^-ing mop.

I used those little symbols because the family newspaper couldn't use the exact word, but I'm pretty sure it's a good guess.

Ms. Herb explained to the police that the toilet had over-flowed and was leaking into the kitchen when she loudly called for a mop. A @#$%^ -ing mop, to be exact.

Her next-door neighbor, hearing this agonized plea for help, didn't get off his @#$%^-ing ass to help her, say, with a plunger in his hand, but rather reported the cursing to the police who showed up to give her a citation.

Along with possible jail time, she was told that she could be ordered to pay a fine of $300, which could be better used to pay for roughly three minutes of a plumber's time, if you ask me.

So, why does this sad tale from many states away give me the shivers?

Simple. I live in a ninety-year-old house and I know what it's like to stand in highly questionable water every now and then. And by highly questionable, I mean shitalicious.

The last time this happened, I seem to recall saying some-thing on the order of "Oopsie daisy! This silly goose of a toilet is overflowing all over the floor. Let me just shut the water off and grab a few towels! It's no big deal!"

No, wait! That's not what I said at all. It was more of a "Oopsie @#$%^-ing daisy! This @#$%^-ing toilet is over-flowing all over the @#$%^-ing place. Let me just shut the mother@#$%^-ing water off and grab a few @#$%^-ing towels. This is a big @#$%^-ing deal."

Fortunately, my neighbors didn't report this outburst for a couple of reasons: They have ninety-year-old plumbing themselves and were probably busy cussing out their own toilets and, let's see, what else? Oh, yes! They are not complete morons.

I dunno about y'all, but I've cussed out every appliance in my house at one time or the other. The time-honored tradition of cussing out appliances is as American as magnetic car ribbons.

The @#$%^-ing food processor usually gets the worst of it, followed closely by the @#$%^-ing vacuum cleaner. They're a couple of @#$%^-ing assholes, those two.

I also feel sorry for Ms. Herb because she said the cursing began while trying to get her daughter to hear her cries for a mop.

Having both a toilet and a daughter of my own, I can say with absolute certainty that the daughter was probably listening to her @#$%^-ing iPod and wouldn't have noticed unless the toilet had physically propelled itself off its wax seal and lurched into her bedroom right by itself to demand a little help.

At which point, the daughter would just close her eyes tight and scream: "Mooooooommmmm! The @#$%^-ing toilet is in my room again."

Now who's screaming for help?

People are just too @#$%^-ing sensitive these days, if you ask me. Consider the case, also from up north, New Hampshire to be precise, where four town hall employees were fired for gossiping.

One fired employee was probably puzzled about being fired for gossiping about the boss's cozy relationship with another employee. After all, she admitted to casually calling him "the führer" to his face without any ill effects.

This means that he would apparently rather be compared to Hitler, the greatest mass murderer in history, than to be accused of spending too long talking about last night's episode of *Two and a Half Men* with the cute chick in accounting.

Go @#$%^-ing figure!

Digging deeper, I learned that this Podunk town in New Hampshire wasn't the only place where you could be fired for gossiping.

Turns out, just an hour or so from my North Carolina home, liquor store employees in a neighboring county can be fired for gossiping, thanks to a new rule enacted by the county commissioners.

They're all wife swappers, by the way. What? What'd I say? Everybody knows that.

I'm just guessing, but this probably stems from some busybody blabbing about the holiness preacher buying bourbon one day and him not even seeming to have any semblance of a stubborn cough.

Growing up in a very small North Carolina town, I was always amused at the fortresslike protective wall around the front and sides of the local liquor store. Once parked in the back, you could scurry inside in utter shame and, a few minutes later, scurry back out, brown paper bags in hand, without the threat of gossipy biddies seeing your every move and reporting it back to the loaves-and-fishes committee.

Perhaps similar walls could be erected between offices with employees forced to navigate *Survivor*-style mazes to get to another's cubicle for a little harmless flirtation to break up the day.

Having worked in a cubicle environment for more than two decades, I can promise you that gossip is absolutely essential to the mental health of an employee. Without it, well, you'd just work all day and that's too @#$%^-ing horrible to contemplate.

Gossip doesn't have to ruin lives to be fun, although that is an added bonus if it's about somebody you really can't stand.

This is America, after all, and we have the right to free speech. And if that speech happens to be about the boss's porn addiction, so what?

I was telling someone about my outrage at people being fined for cussing and fired for gossiping, and you know what she said? "It is what it is."

Well, yes, what else would it be? This has got to be the most overused, idiotic expression since "It's all good."

Even my plumber used it recently, now that I think about it. I shoulda given him a piece of my @#$%^-ing mind.

Listen in, with my permission, of course. . . .

Me: "I think the flapper's busted; what do you think?"

Plumber: "It is what it is."

Me: "What the hell does that mean?"

An hour later, the toilet is repaired and the bill is presented. I give the plumber a check that isn't signed.

Plumber: "You forgot to sign the check, ma'am."

Me: "Oh, did I? Well, it is what it is."

Plumber: "Well what it *is* is an unsigned check."

Me: "It's all good."

Plumber: "Not without your signature it's not."

Ha! I got him! It's my birthday! It's my birthday! (OK, also overused. I envision spending my golden years at the Old Clichés Home where I can sit with my friends on the front porch and cheerfully say things like "Word" and "Not!" and "My bad" without shame.)

The expression "It is what it is" is almost always accompanied by a heavy sort of world-weary sigh and pregnant pause so that all this McWisdom can have time to sink in. It's as if pearls have spilled from the lips of Socrates his own self. Socrates Jones, maybe.

And it's everywhere.

Persnickety diner: "This is iceberg lettuce, but the menu clearly said romaine."

Waiter (with light shrug and gentle smile): "It is what it is."

Patient: "Doctor, I can't believe you amputated the wrong leg!"

Doc (wry smile): "I know. But really, what can I say? It is what it is."

Patient: "What it *is* is a malpractice suit."

Doc: "Bingo."

Judge: "You've confessed to stabbing, shooting, and setting fire to at least a dozen of your friends and family members. What do you have to say for yourself?"

Defendant: "Your Honor, it is what it is."

Judge: "Right you are! And because of your impeccable logic and insight, you are free to go!"

"It is what it is" replaces former irritant "I'm not saying anything, I'm just saying."

Whaaa?

This is usually a prelude to something that is going to be pretty harsh. Just as we bless the heart in the South before we remove it from your chest and stomp on it.

So to recap: It is in fact *not* all good. You are, too, saying something and "It is what it is" makes no @#$%^-ing sense.

Don't agree with me? Too bad. That's just how I roll.

Oops.

18

Lessons Taught Here

My daddy was a retired public school teacher. He spent a lifetime teaching other people's kids.

OK, not really a lifetime. He took up teaching after jobs as a sewing machine repairman and work at the textile mill in town didn't pan out. He'd been the only person in his family to go to college but, when he got out, for reasons I never understood, he trotted his degree from Wake Forest College right on over to the textile mill that employed practically every family in town in the business of weaving fabric for car-seat covers.

The mill was a powerful lure, perhaps because you got every Fourth of July week off and there was a huge family Christmas party, for all the "lintheads" and their kids, with bologna and pineapple kabobs that made us feel sort of chic. We were like characters in our beloved *Bewitched*. At the party, we spent just a few magical moments standing mere inches away from the plant manager and his wife, whose flipped bob was so reminiscent of Samantha Stephens' that we knew we were in the presence of *classy people*. The kind of people who eat little chocolate-glazed marshmallows on toothpicks and know how to mix a proper Manhattan or twelve.

The mill's Christmas party was the second biggest thing to happen in our little town around the holidays, the first being the delivery of a twelve-pack of assorted pickles from the folks at the oil company that filled up the tank behind the house. There was another oil company in town but they only gave you a calendar with a photo of a blond-headed little girl all dressed up for church and praying in front of a stained-glass window. Nobody much used their heating oil.

The pickle box was gigantic and provided enough bread-and-butters, gherkins, dill chips, midgets, spears, and relish to last the whole year. We awaited delivery of the pickle box like the Cratchits dreaming of a real turkey instead of one made only of old socks and hope.

After the mill, there was a brief stint selling burial insurance for quarter-a-month premiums that meant Daddy was home a lot during the day, and at night would sometimes return with little prizes for my sister and me.

Thumb-sized six-packs of wax bottles filled with "fruit" juice you drank before eating the wax bottle were the best, followed closely by pink-tipped candy "cigarettes."

Remember that cigarettes were not only in fashion; they

were the perfect pretend accessory for a second grader like me. "Yes, Darrin, I'll have another Manhattan, and would you mind lighting my ciggie? What?! It's already lit! That would explain the hot-pink burning ash. Tra-la-laaaaa."

Somewhere in there, my daddy worked briefly for the Internal Revenue Service. He had a desk and a spinning chair but had to drive a twenty-year-old car a hundred miles a day round trip on roads that hadn't improved since wagon-train days.

Once he finally decided to try teaching, he realized that you only got paid nine months out of the year, so he did what a lot of teachers did and sold *World Book Encyclopedia*s from door to door.

This was a fabulous job as far as my sister and I were concerned because every salesman got to take home a World Book cyclorama game, a sort of early Trivial Pursuit that was cool and made entirely of plastic.

With a jar of chilled oil-company dill spears, a few packs of pink-tipped "cigarettes" and cyclorama to keep us company, our summer was set.

I don't think Daddy ever sold many sets of *World Book*. When he did sell a few, we nervously waited to make sure the check had cleared and he could collect his commission before we could celebrate. If it didn't clear, the encyclopedias would have to be picked back up and I imagined forlorn, over-alled country kids with many missing teeth saying, "Please, Mister, I ain't gotten past aardvark and there's a big ol' world out there!"

By the time fall and winter rolled around, and monthly paychecks were back in play, our thoughts turned only to pickles, and lots of 'em.

But one dark Christmas, the pickle box didn't come. In a stunning slap in the face to original thought, the new owners of the oil company had the nerve to present each customer instead with the blond girl with the praying hands and stained-glass window calendar.

I wanted to slap her, even though obviously it wasn't her fault. She was just some Midwestern photographer's cute little girl (although, if I was right, she was probably in her mid-forties by now) and knew nothing of the pickle angst that was being felt across the land. OK, not the land, but at least about twenty square miles of scrub pine and substandard housing in southeastern North Carolina.

Teachers had tons of time off at Christmas, perhaps because Jesus had been one. He hadn't worked in a textile mill, obviously, so you only got one week a year.

I could only hope that the oil company didn't get any vacation at all. They had given and taketh away and I was irrationally disappointed as Christmas after Christmas passed pickleless.

By the time I got to high school, Daddy was teaching at the same high school.

"You in your dad's class?" people would ask.

Since he taught special education, I had to say that I wasn't. He was small-framed but strong like most Rivenbark men, and had the ability, also like Rivenbark men, to turn perfectly tan in less time than it would take to walk shirtless to the edge of his garden, pluck a warm tomato, and bite into it.

Having inherited the, uh, delicate porcelain skin of my mother's side of the family, I could only seethe as I lay on a sweaty webbed chaise longue day after day reading *Tiger Beat* and turning watermelon pink before peeling.

Daddy's students all towered over him but he was proud of having never had to send one to the office.

"Not one time," he would say much later, after I was married and the mother of a fifth grader myself. "Never sent one to the office. Not once."

At eighty-five, he had slowed considerably and now I was learning all about something called dementia.

Suddenly, or so it seemed, he was staring in wonder at the speed with which I could tie his shoes after a doctor's appointment.

"You do that good," he'd say, looking down while I worked on these funny saddle oxfords that were his favorite shoes in the world.

"It's not rocket science," I muttered under my breath, tired of answering the same question twenty times in the past hour. Instantly, I felt a wave of guilt for being so snotty-sounding.

"You do that good," he repeated. He might say it a few more times, this I knew. Sometimes, he repeated things so often I thought I would lose my own mind, joining him in this place where he had gone.

I knew that, in a few minutes, he would ask me, once

again, to check into some idiot insurance program that a has-been movie star had been advertising on TV lately. I came to nurture a genuine loathing for the has-beens and their rip-off insurance plans.

"You can't be denied for any reason," said my daddy. He said it again, apparently enjoying the feel of the words in his mouth.

Lately, he had taken to humming "Amazing Grace" wherever we went. The grocery store. The cafeteria. Even the doctor's waiting room. The sound was not sweet, I thought, again feeling guilt for not celebrating the comfort that this old hymn seemed to bring him.

I remember thinking that I should be thankful that he could say anything to me at all, even if lately it was the same thing over and over.

And I reminded myself that it's easy to be grateful for the obvious blessings in life, much harder to be grateful for the tough moments and the lessons they teach.

This man, who was down to 106 pounds now, had driven me to every sock hop and sleepover when I was a whiny pre-teen. He taught me how to drive a straight shift, never raising his voice as I lurched and jerked and impatiently ignored his advice.

"You do that good," he had said when I finally, after many weeks and a few tears, mastered the art of parallel parking.

And now, four decades later and able to parallel park and tie shoes successfully, I realized that he was still teaching, even though it wasn't intentional.

He was teaching me how to be a better person, someone less self-absorbed and less in a hurry. I had to slow down when I was with him. I had to breathe deeply. I learned to join him in a simple celebration of a sunny spot on my parents' concrete patio.

"This is nice," he said one day, surveying through eyes dimmed by macular degeneration and a memory that was getting increasingly jumbly. "This is nice."

And it was. His last lesson taught was an appreciation for life stripped down to its barest bones.

And, under my breath, on that sunny spot on the patio, I thought, *You do that good.*

A few days after his memorial service, I did a final errand for my daddy. The funeral home was just a couple of blocks from my house. In the deep, carefully reassuring tones that funeral directors use, they called to say that I could pick up my father's "cremains." It's a word that is at once perfectly descriptive and gruesome.

I walked down the street to the funeral home on possibly the prettiest, most perfect February day I had ever seen. Warm, slight breeze, budding crocuses everywhere. It was as if I was in a splashy musical and all the flowers would bloom and nod and turn colors as soon as I passed by.

Walking back, cradling a box swaddled in purple velvet, I hoped that I wouldn't run into anyone because I didn't really want to have to explain what I was carrying.

But it was too gorgeous a day. The neighbors were out. Considering that it was the middle of the afternoon on a workday, an almost comical number of them stopped me to say hello and a couple of them, yes, asked cheerily, "What's in the box?"

I told them.

"Oh, sorry!"

"No, no, he would've loved taking a stroll on a day like today."

A long time ago, I had a friend whose father died and was cremated. He loved two things in this world, she said: hot dogs and flying. So she put him in her carry-on, flew him to the Charlotte airport, bought a jumbo dog with mustard and relish, put his urn on the little round table, ate half the hot dog and, one hour later, boarded the plane for the hourlong flight home, her daddy stowed safely back in her carry-on.

It was a great story, and walking along with the purple velvet box o' Daddy I thought I knew exactly how she felt sitting in that airport restaurant, toasting her dad with exactly one-half of a cold Bud Lite.

About halfway home, I caught myself humming "Amazing Grace." The sound was sweet.

19

The Wrestler and the Fan

I remember just like it was yesterday the sticky July morning I stole the wrestling poster off the telephone pole and made little Hermie Drucker cry.

Sure, I was twelve and I should've taken the high road. Hermie, the asthmatic redheaded kid brother of a friend of mine, was only seven, and the wail he let out when he pedaled his Western Auto banana bike up to that pole to claim "his" poster could've been heard six counties away.

I could easily hear Hermie's screams of outrage from my post across the road at MacMillan's, a rickety country store with a wood floor so worn out that, to a bare foot, it felt as soft as a satin bedspread. Watching Hermie from underneath the rusty overhang at the Sinclair pumps made me feel a little guilty.

There he was, so full of hope and determination, ready to

rip "our" poster off that telephone pole and skedaddle back home, where he would have, no doubt, taped it to his wall right alongside the Rip Hawk and Swede Hansen poster he'd stolen from me not six months earlier.

Just thinking about it made me mad as a hen on a hot griddle. *Little shit,* I thought, picturing the way the green- and orange- and yellow-striped poster *with photos* would have looked on my own bedroom wall.

Hermie and I both wanted this latest poster, and we finally agreed (me, with my fingers crossed neatly behind my back) that the only Christian thing to do would be to wait until the tag-team match between George Becker and Johnny Weaver at the Wallace National Guard Armory was officially over. Which had been the previous night.

"You snooze, you lose," I shouted to Hermie, who just stared at me as if I had sprouted horns and a forked tail. All that was left on the creosote pole was little bitty pieces of the orange corners of the poster stuck to a few staples that I hadn't been able to dislodge. They mocked him.

Although he was only seven years old, Hermie's apple hadn't fallen far from the evangelistic family tree. His grandmother, a snow-haired woman, four-feet eight inches in height and the same approximate width, had taught the catechism to all the country kids in our dinky little North Carolina town.

"You're going to hell!" Hermie said, now wiping away the beginnings of a tear.

As he stomped his flip-flopped foot pointlessly into a

growth of pop-gums, I watched with increasing amusement, finally catching his eye just long enough to flip him off.

"Hell! Hell! That there just seals the deal!" Hermie hollered.

I'd have to do a good deal of catechism refreshment for loving Hermie's misery so much.

"We had a deal!" he yelled with a fierceness I wasn't altogether expecting. Hanging at his sides, Hermie's fat little fists were balled up so tight it made the freckles disappear right off his knuckles.

I cupped my hand behind my ear and shook my head. I can't hear a word out of your freckly-lipped mouth, I was letting him know. Which, obviously, wasn't the truth at all.

"What's up Hermie's butt?" my friend Deb asked, having maneuvered her bike under the overhang beside mine.

"I got the poster first," I said.

"Don't look like he's taking it too good," she said, causing us both to laugh because now Hermie had taken to jumping up and down on the pop-gums like a damn fool.

"It's mighty hot out, Hermie," I hollered. Deb ripped open a skinny little sleeve of Lance's salted peanuts and, just as we'd done a million times before, poured half the contents of the bag into her Co-Cola and handed me the rest. We switched off and shared like that, first me buying the peanuts and then Deb. This was a concept Hermie was going to have to learn the hard way.

"Shut up!" he said, continuing to stomp and getting redder and redder in the face.

I wasn't sure if seven-year-olds could actually have a stroke, but Hermie looked like he was headed that way.

"Both of y'all need to grow up," said Deb, wiping some stray peanut salt off her cheeks with the back of her hand. "It's just a stupid wrestling match. Who cares anyway?"

Who cares???

Deb, dressed in a ruffly midriff shirt and madras shorts she'd bought with money from priming tobacco, had no time for such pursuits. At fourteen, she was far more interested in finding a boyfriend with a car who she could go "ridin' around" with on Friday night. This is what passed for entertainment back in rural eastern North Carolina in the sixties and seventies, and may still, for all I know.

Maybe wrestling was something I'd grow out of, but I doubted it. My idea of a good time had nothing to do with getting in some fool's car and riding around the Dairi O something like seven hundred times in a row while Steppenwolf howled from the eight-track.

No, when I was twelve, a good time was defined by eating an entire box of Crackin' Good butter cookies (always on sale for fifty-nine cents a box at Winn Dixie) while watching the wrestling matches on TV every Saturday night.

It should be noted that no one in my family shared my passion for wrestling. In fact, the only person in my immediate world who understood how I felt about wrestling was Hermie, an unlikely soul mate who was crying his little heart out.

Looking at the broken little boy, sitting red-faced on a cushion of weeds, I felt like a monster.

A monster with the coolest damn poster of them all. Because I loved George Becker and Johnny Weaver better than all of the other professional wrestlers put together. There had been brief flirtations with others, but George and Johnny were my favorites, and nothing would ever change that.

I wasn't alone in my obsession, or else how could they have raised so many thousands of dollars from truly poor people who would stand in line more than an hour to sit in the sweaty, smelly Armory? Usually it was a fund-raiser with a smallish percentage going to the volunteer fire department to buy a Jaws of Life or maybe the Ruritans' building fund, so you could even say that it was noble to attend these events. Not so noble, perhaps, to shotgun beers out in the parking lot ahead of time like some of the kids did, but nothing's perfect.

I wasn't old enough to go to a wrestling match at the Armory by myself, so I had to settle for watching my heroes on TV. When that nasty little Japanese wrestler (I forget his name on purpose) took out a drawstring bag of salt hidden in the waistband of his shorts and tossed the contents into George and Johnny's eyeballs, I jumped up from my chair, scattering flower-shaped butter cookies all over the oval braided rug on our living room floor.

"Y'all know he's sneaky!" I'd shout, talking to the TV just as if my boys could hear me and correct their behavior.

"Educated people don't watch this sort of thing," my mother huffed as she walked by and scowled at the cookies on the rug. "You know it's all fake, don't you?"

I had an answer for that awful question right ready.

"If it's fake, then why does Dr. Dawes believe in it enough to buy out fifty front-row seats every single time the wrestling comes to the Armory?"

My mother shook her head. She didn't have an answer for that and, frankly, no one else did, either.

Dr. Dawes was as close as you could get to a real, live saint walking and living among us. He healed people and saved lives and birthed so many thousands of babies (me included) that he was even written up as "Tar Heel of the Week" in the Raleigh *News & Observer*.

"You think the Tar Heel of the Week wouldn't know if something was fake or not?" I asked, sensing that I'd found the perfect vulnerable spot.

My mother shrugged sadly and left the room, unable to offer any sort of rational explanation for this man she loved and respected being caught up in something so obviously moronic.

But there sat Dr. Dawes at ringside—I saw it with my own eyes one night when I was in my twenties—the same scrupulously clean and oddly elegant hands that had caught thousands of babies and comforted thousands more sick souls, clenched into fists balled up just like little Hermie Drucker's on that long-ago day. At seventy-five or so, Dr. Dawes shouted, slung popcorn, and all but crawled into the ring himself to right a perceived wrong.

"Settle down, now, Doc," the referee said, trying unsuccessfully not to grin. No doubt, Dr. Dawes had delivered the referee into the world along with anyone else under about the age of fifty that happened to be in the audience.

In the newspaper, it had been noted that Dr. Dawes had "even delivered three sets of Siamese twins!" This was, of course, before political correctness would water that down to the clinical "conjoined twins" that is used today. Face it: When the bad-guy wrestler in the ring with an Asian heritage is nicknamed "The Yeller Menace," it's fairly obvious that no one frets much about racial stereotypes.

The stereotypes were in glorious form in the wrestling ring. Maybe that was the appeal of the whole thing to someone like me who liked everything simple and orderly. The good guys looked good, and the bad guys wore hideous tight masks over their faces and scowled and spat. Good looks helped. Over the years, I switched my shallow loyalties to a wrestler named Mike Rotundo, whom I once drove a hundred miles to see in person at somebody else's crappy National Guard Armory.

Years later, long after little Hermie Drucker had become a highway patrolman much respected by all of the community and I had become a newspaper reporter not respected by much of anybody, I had the chance to go to a wrestling match again. I'd volunteered to do a profile on the state of rural wrestling fund-raisers, arguing that they were practically nonexistent thanks to cable. I'd done something similar on womanless weddings and on people who make clothes out of beer cans and a whole bunch of other Southern anomalies.

"Maybe nobody goes anymore because they finally figured out that it's all fake," said one snooty reporter who had moved south from Connecticut. "It's not like it's a real sport." He put little quote marks in the air when he got to the word "sport."

I chuckled at the image of what this annoying-ass Yankee boy would look like after a few seconds in the ring with my old crush, Mike Rotundo. Stewed squash, that's what.

Showing up with pad and pen, I was going to do something that I was doing a lot of lately, much to the delight of all the Yankee transplants, and that was to tell them about the way it used to be.

Stepping into a pitiful gym with peeling paint, thirtyeight miles from the nearest Starbucks, I watched a young local make his debut in the ring.

He called himself Mean Mike Brash. Trouble was, he wasn't mean at all. Just a very young, pale, and rather slightly built blond-haired boy who thought high school was overrated and was chasing his dream right off the TV screen and into this dilapidated gym. It was for a good cause, as usual. In this case charity began, and ended, at home. Proceeds would help buy paint for the gym.

Thank goodness his tag-team partner, the "Dark Knight," was more savvy. He played to the crowd, pretending to throw a chair at a little girl who screamed and hid behind her eighteen-year-old daddy's skinny legs.

Once the match started, with the good guys wearing red, white, and blue and Mean Mike calling a little bent-over country woman who was booing him from the front row "you toothless ol' hag," I felt right at home.

It had been too long. I forgot about taking notes, savoring the spectacle in front of me and burning my throat with too-salty popcorn.

The little woman balled up her fists in front of her face, just like Dr. Dawes had done so many years ago and, to the amazement of everyone in the gym except her grown son beside her, invited Mean Mike to "come down 'ere and say that, you bastard!"

Was it fake? Real? It mattered not. This was Southern-style wrestling at its essence. And I, for one, knew that the only thing that would make this night more perfect would be a box of butter cookies to eat or, perhaps, to toss into the ring in disgust.

I heard that Mean Mike's career ended shortly after that night, having had to choose between snapping necks and saving souls. He became a gospel singer with a band that played in the very same armories where he'd once called nice people's grandmas toothless ol' hags.

Only in the South, I thought. Happily.

20

No TV? I'll Put My Carbon Footprint Up Your Behind

For some weird reason, I've been getting lots of press releases lately from companies wanting me to use my newspaper column to promote "staycations," sad little close-to-home trips designed to be gentle on your pocketbook. Laudable but dull as hell.

Camping is the ultimate family staycation, they say. Save money in this battered economy! Sleep under the stars and eat food from cans just like Boxcar Willie!

Clearly, the public relations folks at these companies don't know me or they'd realize that sending me a story idea about how to, and I am not making this up, "cook on a mountainside in the worst conditions" is a huge mistake. The words "vacation" and "worst conditions" go together like Barack Obama and plaid flannel.

Then there was the "urgent media advisory" from the

makers of a handheld bug-repelling device that "efficiently repels black flies, mosquitoes, and no-see-um's." You know what else repels those insects? Hotel rooms. Big, sumptuous hotel rooms with windows that are sealed shut to prevent some dumbass from jumping and beds that don't brag about having "a chest-high heat baffle and forehead comfort tube." I refuse to take a vacation or staycation where, rather than contemplate the supreme joy that comes with an impossibly high thread count, I must fumble for a blow-up pillow that looks and smells like a kid's swim ring. The camp bed boasts a "silken" lining. That's right; just like a *casket*.

Sure, who'd want a real vacation at some seaside cottage with panoramic views, plasma TVs, and nifty portable wine cellars in every room?

Why would I want that sort of comfort when I could embrace the great outdoors? With my trusty stainless-steel multitool, the absolute latest in versatile camping knick-knacks, I can not only open a can of cold beef stew but also use the handy hook on one end to disembowel a bear.

Speaking of bears, one press release reminded campers to always hang all foodstuffs high in the trees so as not to tempt the wildlife. You know where wild animals won't walk up and try to take your supper from you? Restaurants, that's where. Think about it. When's the last time you actually saw a hungry coyote strolling through the lobby at Ruth's Chris? Plus, they're probably too stupid to order the bread pudding once they get there. You know coyotes.

Another press release reminded me that staycationers should invest in a portable navigation system. These are especially useful for campers who can't find their ass in the dark with both hands and a flashlight.

They're waterproof, have a built-in compass, and are small enough to fit in your hand, conveniently leaving the other hand for waving good-bye to any hope of ever seeing your family again. I have a favorite navigation system, too. It's called a *pilot*.

Strolling hand in hand with the staycation movement is the green movement, but as Kermit said years ago, it ain't easy being green.

A good friend sent me a very earnest e-mail asking our family to participate in something called "earth hour." I did a double take when I read the hour that had been chosen for people to "not use any power, but rather spend the time changing out old non-Al Gore—sanctioned lightbulbs or brainstorming with family members on ways to reduce emissions and live more sustainably."

God almighty, Saturday night ain't what it used to be.

While the idea of "earth hour" is probably laudable, I had to wonder who in his right mind would plan a voluntary power blackout on the night of the NCAA regional finals. Sounded to me like someone had been smoking his eco-friendly hemp pillowcases. If they'd pulled the plug on my TV that night, I'd have left my carbon footprint up somebody's behind.

It was hard enough trying to live through the TV writers'

strike, so I basically keep it on twenty-four/seven now just out of gratitude. Naturally, I took the side of the writers because, technically, I are one. They are my brethren and sisteren. And, yeah, I know that brethren isn't a real word.

I can't be asked to turn off the TV for any length of time, not even for the sake of the planet. What if I were to miss a "very special episode" of anything? During the writers' strike, even the little TiVo icon who lives inside my TV and is normally so bouncy and happy looked as if he needed Zoloft.

No, I couldn't turn off the TV or, as another "greenie" suggested, cut back on the number of viewing hours. I was still healing from that writers' strike which, being raised in the South, I didn't even understand. Southerners don't know a lot about unions. In fact, my entire education on the organized labor movement came from watching *Norma Rae* eleventy billion times. It's why Paula Deen, Southern icon, had no idea that it wasn't cool to cross a picket line at Smithfield Foods, which basically pays its workers in lottery tickets and honey buns. Poor Paula. All those loud agitators dressed as bacon strips yelling at her when all she wanted to do was sit around and talk with her irrationally handsome sons about the best way to tenderize gizzards. None of 'em would know a picket line from a picket fence, if you ask me.

The TV writers' strike meant there was more reality TV clogging the airwaves than ever because they didn't require real writers. There's no need for witty banter because it's all formulaic. Like how Heidi Klum bends over and mutters "auf Wiedersehen" into the ear of whatever doomed *Project Runway* contestant has to pack up her knives and leave Trump Tower (sorry, they all run together in my head). I'm pretty sure that's German for "Your designs suck rocks. No, really, they do." But the contestants don't speak German, natch, so they have no idea that this is something that Heidi and Seal will laugh about later while their many children clamber about them for yet another magazine photo op.

Here's the thing: As long as it doesn't involve turning off my TV, I want to be green because it seems like a cute, trendy thing to do but, let's be honest, "sustainably harvested caviar" is expensive and I don't really want a wind turbine in my backyard because it would clash with the big-as-shit blow-up swimming pool from Target that millions of tiny polypropylenes already gave their lives for.

I like my store-bought Dove soap and I don't want to make my own by gathering and boiling horse chestnut flowers on account of *I'm not Amish.*

And sure it's sad that Americans toss twenty-five thousand *tons* of toothbrushes into landfills every year, but chewing bark and swishing with saltwater hasn't worked since, like, Sacagawea.

My eco-geek friend named Mountain says I should be more concerned about the dangers of off-gassing, which is what happens when materials that are filled with volatile organic compounds release gaseous pollutants into the air.

"We breathe off-gases even when we sleep," said Mountain,

while I had to wonder how she knew so much about my husband.

Mountain paused to pull a tube of beeswax lipstick made from cruelty-free hives in the Amazon from her $285 organic cotton shorts.

If I suggest a drugstore lipstick that would last a lot longer, she scowls at me as if I had personally tested "just peachy" on a caged baboon my own self.

Of course, even the most well-intentioned greenies have to realize that the movement has jumped the shark when ads encourage you to ditch your perfectly good old TV so you can buy a pricier one that's "green" only because it's trimmed in "renewable bamboo." Nah, that's not wasteful.

I'm sick to death of all the catalogs promoting "green" living-room furniture, "green" kitchenware, and "green" clothing. Guess where all your old shit goes when you go on that eco-shopping spree. That's right. Mr. Landfill. See? I care about the planet. Just not when Carolina plays.

The only thing I find even less appealing than staycations and the eco-friendly obsession is running. Don't get me wrong. I've always rather admired runners for their dedication to the sport, rising early to jog for perhaps miles all in the name of improving their cardiovascular health and overall fitness.

My own precious duh-hubby is a runner, getting up in the dark every morning to gallop through our neighborhood (which looks a lot like the *Thriller* video at that hour, now that I think about it), taking great care not to wake me on his way out the door.

Just as I detest camping, fitness isn't high on the list, either. I prefer to watch physical exertion from a safe distance, say a nice outdoor café where I can smile encouragingly at passing triathlon participants whilst wiping chocolate croissant glaze off my mouth.

"See ya, wouldn't wanna be ya," runs in a cheerful little singsong loop inside my noggin, though I would be the first to admit this is born of laziness and sloth, and I know that Runners Are Better People.

I have several close friends who have run marathons, a word that is actually derived from two Swahili words: *mara*, which means "to die a horrible death," and *thon*, which means "for a stupid T-shirt." Look it up.

Marathon runners squirt little packets of brown gel into their mouths every few miles to give themselves a burst of protein. I'll join them as soon as they can condense that to tiny little lasagna casseroles.

They speak of endorphins released and something called "runner's high," which just seems like so much trouble. Wouldn't it be easier to just sit around and sip some yummy Firefly Sweet Tea-Flavored Vodka. (Talk about your marriages made in heaven, or, in the case of the Firefly brand, a little island near Charleston, South Carolina. Firefly works for me, and you don't even sweat. Much.)

Nearly everyone I know runs, either in the morning or at night after work.

I know this because now that it gets dark earlier, I almost hit a few of them while trying to back my car out of the driveway. I wish they'd move.

But you know who I really admire? The Arizona jogger who I read about recently. She was attacked by a rabid fox and continued her run for another mile with the animal's jaws *clamped onto her arm.* She told deputies that she was jogging along a favorite trail when a fox jumped out and bit her leg. So she calmly lifted up the fox by its neck and kept running with the varmint clinging to her arm.

Wearing that fox wrapped around her like it was one of those glassy-eyed fur stoles that elderly church ladies used to wear, the jogger was determined to take the fox with her and have it tested for rabies. She jogged the last mile back to her car, tossed the foamy fox into the trunk, and drove to the hospital.

Now I don't know about y'all, but if I'm out for a jog and a rabid animal latches onto me, there will be no need for testing on account of *I will already have dropped dead* from the sheer horror of it all.

The world's bravest woman had to start a series of rabies shots, and so did the poor animal control officer who got bit trying to get the varmint out of the car.

I believe we can all agree on one thing: Running can kill you. Pass the croissants.

Here, in honor of my friend Michelle, who just ran her first half marathon, is her favorite meal when she camps out. I prefer to cook it indoors like God and Kenmore by Sears intended. It's a tried-and-true recipe that perfectly illustrates the curious Southern ability to create shockingly tasty meals with canned ingredients. I call it . . .

MICHELLE'S BELLY-BUSTIN' SUPER SUPPER

This is a nice way to sober up quickly if you have overindulged in the aforementioned Firefly vodka during the cocktail hour. Listen, y'all: Run, do not stagger, to your local likker store and ask if they've got Firefly yet. If not, demand that they look into it, and yesterday. This unspeakably delicious hooch is going to replace the mint julep as the Southerner's "getcher drunk on" beverage of choice; just watch. Drink it on the rocks, if you're brave, but I prefer it mixed with two parts spring water, lemonade, or orangeade. Garnish with mint or lemon and orange wedges if you're feeling show-offy. Simply the best, I do declare.

1 can corn
1 can kidney beans
1 can black beans
1 can diced tomatoes
1 can refried beans
2 cups water

1 envelope ranch dressing mix
1 envelope taco seasoning

Don't drain any of the canned stuff; just pour all the ingredients into a big pot and heat through. If you want to get "faincy," you can garnish with shredded cheese and sour cream and serve it with a big ol' bag of blue-corn tortilla chips.

21

Checkerboard Dreams:
Shaggin' with the (Sorta) Stars

When they asked me to participate in a *Dancing with the Stars* shag competition in Myrtle Beach, I was flattered but exceedingly nervous.

Myrtle Beach, South Carolina, to those of you who haven't ventured this far south, is the shag capital of the world, possibly the universe. If they shag on Neptune, we'd kick their two-headed asses, those of us who have danced on the red-and-white checkerboard floor of Studebaker's, the holy shrine of the serious shagger. Shag, you see, is the official dance of the Carolinas. With its history rooted in jitterbug and jump blues, shag is always danced to R&B—flavored songs, with the legs and feet doing all the fancy moves. It's spectacular to watch and terrifying to master.

That said, being asked to compete in a shag contest in Myrtle Beach is like being asked if you'd like to take a little spin behind the wheel at Talladega or hang out on the balcony at the Vatican.

My bigheaded moment was short-lived, however, after I giddily told a girlfriend that I'd been asked to compete.

"You're in *Dancing with the Stars*?" Pearl asked, acting way too surprised for my taste. "Which star do you get to dance with?"

"What? No! I'm the star!" I corrected her.

"Damn," said Pearl. "They must've exhausted the B-, C-, and D-list celebs. Couldn't they get Debby Boone or Tiffany or somebody?"

Come to think of it, Pearl and I really aren't all that close.

It took a while for me to explain to Pearl that this wasn't *the Dancing with the Stars* with Tom Bergeron and that pretty woman with the man-voice, but rather a charity fund-raiser with the same format. Still, the stakes were high because it was Myrtle Beach. This wasn't some little talent contest at the Moose Lodge; this was the big leagues.

I would be paired with a champion shag dancer by the name of Brad, or as I prefer to call him, the most patient man on earth.

I was terrified but Brad, who had a wall full of trophies but didn't act like it, put me at ease. He was sweet and kind and looked exactly like a grown-up Opie Taylor. We hit it off immediately.

I told Brad that I had never shagged in my life, which was incredibly embarrassing since I was raised just an hour from Carolina Beach, North Carolina, the true birthplace of shag.

Brad, ever the optimist, said he'd much rather work with a clean slate because "that way, there won't be any bad habits ingrained."

Not to worry there. My slate wasn't just clean; it was boiled and bleached and shrink-wrapped. Brad had a huge task ahead of him.

It took about two minutes into our first lesson for me to realize that eighteen months of ballroom dance lessons with hubby weren't going to help at all.

Shag is its own art form. You can't compare it to anything else. Just because you've managed to learn a decent waltz, fox-trot, and rumba doesn't mean anything.

Great shag dancers barely move their torsos throughout the dance; the real action is below the hips, with lots of convoluted kicks and impossible footwork.

Anywho, just learning the basic step took the entire first hour of our lessons. How did Jane Seymour learn to samba in five days? How did God make the world in seven?

I took back all those nasty things I'd said about Jerry Springer's cha-cha. I was even ashamed of saying that woman had a man-voice.

For three months, Brad and I met once or twice a week in the finished room over his garage. We were joined by Sam Cooke, the Temptations, the Reverend Al Green, and Brad's huge yellow lab dog, Jeb, who regarded my pitiful efforts with a baleful look punctuated by the occasional fart, which was pretty much the same reaction I expected from the judges.

Brad demonstrated classic shag moves like the "boogie walk," where your legs go all noodley, and the pivot, a full-speed twirly thing that's scarier than the words "President Jeb Bush."

Because it's actually a judged competition with me and a few other "stars" going for a trophy, I was plenty nervous and had already figured that if things got too bad, I could always faint like Marie Osmond.

Incidentally, if you're talking about participating in a "shag" contest with someone from Great Britain, they might look at you funny because, as anyone who watched *Austin Powers* movies knows, that's the word they use for doing the nasty. So you should try to avoid saying things like, "I told my husband that I was too tired for sex after I'd just spent two hours shagging with Brad in his garage."

See? It just wouldn't sound right.

After all that practice, Brad had come to realize that I would never, ever be able to master the boogie walk and a few other truly tricky maneuvers that would have wowed the judges. The pivot? Nailed it. But the rest of the moves were tougher'n woodpecker lips and I depended on Brad to distract the judges with fancy moves while I would just work the basic step and make sure I didn't move my torso.

Driving down to Myrtle Beach on the afternoon of the contest's date, I was nervous as a hen on a hot griddle. After weeks of listening and debating, Brad and I agreed that "our song" would be that fabulous classic, "Gone Fishin'" by General Johnson and the Chairmen of the Board. Brad was, naturally, too kind to say it, but I knew that one reason he liked it was because it was relatively slow and mercifully brief.

I've danced to "Black Coffee in Bed" before and it's the longest six minutes and twelve seconds of your life.

The good news was that I finally made an actual contribution to the choreography by adding a little twist at the end where I pretended to "reel" Brad toward me with an imaginary fishing pole and he boogie-walked toward me. We took to naming every step something special, and this one was "the crowd pleaser." We might blow up like a squirrel in a microwave out there on the dance floor, but at least everybody would remember our reelin'-in finale. I hoped.

I arrived an hour early and saw Brad dancing on the floor with another one of the championship winners, and my jaw dropped. When he was in his element, on this historic checkerboard floor with a proper partner, he wasn't just a nice guy: He was a rock star.

It was *Dirty Dancing* and he was Patrick Swayze, *Saturday Night Fever* and he was John Travolta.

He saw me and motioned to me to come over so we could practice on the famous floor and dance out the jitters.

It didn't work.

We practiced again, out of sight of the judges, on a little upstairs dance floor between some pool tables. We were wearing coordinating black outfits and I had borrowed Brad's fiancée's fabulously expensive shag shoes.

I have never been more nervous in my life than when the

judges called us together to announce the dance order, decided by simply picking names out of a hat.

For months, Brad had told me he always managed to land
the first dance position; it was positively eerie how it happened. I was hoping his streak would hold because it's much
less intimidating to go first.

I wilted a little as names were called out and we were in
the next-to-last spot. It was going to be a long night. I began
to hate charity.

Brad and I would follow a "star" who had just been named
South Carolina Coach of the Year. He was a huge, charis-
matic bear of a guy who had been in the hospital for a virus
the week before and had loudly announced that he hadn't
eaten solid foods in a week.

Suh-weet.

As we watched the coach dance from our balcony practice nook, I contemplated giving up eating altogether. If this
was what happened after seven days in the hospital on an IV,
I'd hate to see this guy with a few T-bones in him.

"Look at him! He's not sick at all!"

"Don't worry," Brad said, steady as always. "You're gonna
do great; just relax."

I was working on a slight case of bitter because I'd
watched another couple dance earlier and realized that nobody else in the competition was a total novice like me. One
"star" had held the title of Miss Sun Fun, which defines true
royalty in Myrtle Beach. She was sensational and there

wasn't a doubt in my mind that she'd been shagging for most of her life.

At this point, reality sank in. Expectations were lowered. I knew we wouldn't take home the trophy, but I'd just try not to embarrass Brad. Truthfully, my money was on the twinkle-toed coach of the year.

The announcer called our names and Brad and I walked onto the checkerboard floor, hand in hand. He leaned over and whispered "Just have a good time" in my ear.

But it was terrifying. I heard the music, the spotlight found us, and it became sickeningly obvious that we weren't in Brad's room over the garage anymore. Jeb was nowhere to be seen, just sweet duh-hubby and my friends Shirley and Jean Lee heading a small but vocal cheering section.

There was a huge TV screen so the audience could see us no matter where they were sitting. I was fairly certain I was going to throw up on the checkerboards.

"This is worse than childbirth," I whispered back to Brad, who smiled his big, most winning Opie Taylor smile for the judges and said through his teeth: "You're gonna be great."

The rest, as they say, is a blur. I remember nailing the first pivot, forgetting the next two moves we'd choreo-graphed and having Brad pull me closer to whisper me back onto the right count. ("One and two, three and four, five-six . . .") Through it all, I smiled nonstop because someone had told me that, when in doubt, try to look like you're hav-ing a good time.

And then, somehow, two-and-a-half minutes later, it was over. Duh was clapping like crazy and I loved him for that.

The judges were kind and didn't fart even once. Still, I'm a competitive sort and I knew that we weren't in the top three. I didn't want to let Brad down; he'd worked so hard. We finished, I'd say, about seventh out of ten dancers, although nobody really kept score beyond the top three.

I headed back to my cheering section, hugged hubby, and downed a whiskey sour pretty much in one gulp.

They called us all back onto the floor and presented us with very cool black etched trophies shaped like stars.

The Coach of the Year won the big trophy and bragging rights, to nobody's real surprise.

Walking back to our hotel room, which had a great oceanfront view that was pretty even on a freezing January night, Duh told me that he couldn't believe I'd danced at the "shrine" in front of hundreds of people. It was so not like me to do anything so completely out of my comfort zone.

Duh and I go way back, twenty-four years to be exact, and during those years, he's seen me shrink from all sorts of things just because I couldn't stand the thought of risking failure or embarrassment.

Now I had risked both, suffered a little bit of both, survived it all and even, in a crazy sort of way, enjoyed it.

"Would you do it again?" hubby asked, expecting a completely different answer.

I looked him dead in the eye.

"Oh, hell yeah."

22

Get Yer Wassail On;
It's Carolin' Time

This year I really wanted to do the homemade Christmas cookie thing. I've been shamed by the fit young mom down the street who bakes from scratch and is always outside stringing lights and decorating with her kids this time of year. The rest of the year, you see her building forts with them or goofing around on a tire swing. When you ask her what she's up to, she just says, "We're making memories!"

All this time, I just thought her cable wasn't working. Turns out she does all this stuff on purpose.

In a distant chamber inside my coal-black heart, I've always wanted to do some of that corny holiday stuff; I just lack the natural ability. I pictured myself as Martha Stewart's shorter, fatter sister—the one she would've called "Stumpy" with that refined throaty Connecticut accent of hers.

"Oh, look, everyone! Stumpy is here to show us how to

dip pretzels in a bowl of microwaved chocolate. Wow! What will she think of next?"

This year, I decided that Sophie and I would use her Christmas break to make homemade treats from our very own kitchen. I mean, if thousands of meth addicts can do it, why can't we?

I giddily purchased my version of homemade Christmas cookies—rolls of refrigerated cookie dough prestamped with wreaths, Santas, and reindeer heads.

These cookies *so* rock, y'all. Anyone can make them. The instructions on the package prove it: "Remove presliced cookies from roll. Do not slice them. They are presliced. Idiot. Continue to breathe in and out. Place *presliced* cookies on rectangular pan."

Like a Christmas miracle, in nine to twelve minutes, you've got genuine home-baked Christmas cookies. I say "home-baked" because I believe in truth in advertising. I love the TV commercial that shows the happy mom and daughter preparing "place-and-bake" cookies that are packaged one cookie to a slot, a relief for the lobotomized Christmas revelers who find the whole presliced thing too complicated.

After we baked the cookies and let them cool a little as the package directed "because if you eat hot cookies, it could hurt your stupid throat," Soph and I considered doing something else traditional. This year we'd join the memory-making mom, who was, once again, organizing the entire neighborhood to go caroling and "a-wassailing."

"A-what?" I asked her.

"Wassailing! It's an authentic colonial punch! I'm going to make it from scratch and the boys are going to help me."

The notion of eating or drinking anything that had been prepared, even in part, by "the boys" was terrifying to me as I had once seen both of them happily share queso dip from a bowl with the dog.

Pass.

"We'll come over in time to sing," I said.

"Okeydoke," she said, chipper as always. "Whatever floats yer boat! And speaking of boats, the boys and I are going to decorate our sailboat for the holiday flotilla. Would you all like to join us? I've already used a jigsaw to cut out a manger scene and we just have to paint it and wire it. Making memories!"

"Making me sick!" I said under my breath, but she had moved on.

Believe it or not, I'm a huge fan of caroling. If you're a terrible singer or if you have a hard time remembering the words to your favorite Christmas carols, it's important to make up for these two shortcomings by singing very loudly.

Admit it: Past a certain age, we mortals are incapable of remembering whether Frosty's hat was made of felt or silk or if that incredibly annoying little drummer boy's drum goes "rah-pum-pa-pa-bum" or "ma ma se, ma ma sa, ma *mah* coo sa" or something else all together.

In the end, all that matters when caroling is that you sing lustily, filled with the joy of the season and perhaps a few pomegranate martinis if you're the shy type.

The truth is, almost no one gets the lyrics to holiday songs right. It's OK when you're trying to fake "I Saw Mommy Kissing Santa Claus"; less so when you're supposed to be giving reverent attention to "It Came Upon a Midnight Clear."

I've butchered that last one pretty badly.

It came upon a midnight clear
That glorious night of old
With angels bending near the earth
To touch their harps of gold
Peace Out! They said from their, er, holy homes . . .

And it just got worse from there.

Ditto "Away in a Manger," which always stumps me with its mention of cattle "lowing," whatever that means. I find it useful to toss in random "nigh's" when in doubt: "Bless all the dear children in Thy tender care/And nigh and far and nigh, nigh, nigh."

Trust me. *No* one will notice.

One of my very favorite Christmas carols is "What Child Is This?", but I've long forgotten the words. Which is why I knew that when we sang carols with Miss Thang and the Dog Tongue Twins, it would end up sounding like this:

What child is this
Who lays in bed
While shepherds wa-atch, uh, a little TV . . .

Singing in public tip: Usually, if you can just hang on until the chorus, things will click back into a safe zone. This is why you must sing the chorus extraloud, because you're now in familiar territory.

This! This! Is Christ the king,
Whom angels love and leopards ring!"

See how easy?

What you don't want to do is mix your sacred and your Rudolph because, like believing that Santa wraps, this is just plain wrong.

O holy night, the stars are brightly shining
It is the night on the roof, reindeer pause . . .

It makes sense that we'd botch lyrics to songs we only enjoy once a year. Face it; there are still a lot of people who sing, "I'm the God of Velveeta, honey."

Fortunately, Christmas is the season of forgiveness. As long as you remember the names of Rudolph's pals—Donner, Blitzen, Vixen, Cupid, Comet, Dasher, Prancer, and Craig, you'll be fine.

I never miss a Christmas Eve service at our church and get a kick out of the folks who only come once a year, survey the overflowing pews, and tell the ushers they "need four seats together" like they're at a ballet recital or a Little League game.

Because there are three services, the ushers often say to come back for the next one and arrive early to claim a pew.

"That doesn't work for us," they'll say, looking pained while consulting watches that cost more than my car. Then they lower eyeglasses and stare at the ushers as if this is a point that can be negotiated.

This entitlement of the come-late set owes to the fact that way back in the day a long-dead ancestor who actually went to church every Sunday bought and paid for the stained-glass windows in the sanctuary. So there.

As they greet another family they haven't seen in fifty-two weeks, they are quick to put to good use that most practiced of all phrases that rich old Southern families love best.

"Mutha and Fatha bought the children the most gawjus sweatahs for Crusmus."

They have stood in front of mirrors and practiced this phrase over and over until it is Southern old-money perfection. If it can be said without moving the lips even a smidgen, all the better.

My guess is they didn't order a single gift from the white-trash Christmas catalogs that overflow my mailbox every year. They are less Horchow and more dog chow with their offerings of battery-operated dogs and cats that breathe and snore.

You can also order a vaguely disturbing Christmas tree ornament from your dead relative inscribed: "I love you all dearly, now don't shed a tear, I'm spending my Christmas with Jesus this year." Since one costs twenty dollars and two are only twenty-five dollars, you should probably wait for two relatives to die to take advantage of this one.

These catalogs seem to be targeted to a very specific buyer: people obsessed with door drafts (plain and dachshund-shaped "draft dodgers" are sold); people with webbed feet (else, why so many "toe separators"?); people who obsess about the storage and laundering of their ball cap collection; people who prefer the look and feel of transparent plastic on their carpet, couches, and dining-room chairs; women obsessed with securing wayward bra straps and storing and transporting devilled eggs; people who are inexplicably proud to display many rolls of toilet paper on various metal scrolled thingies; people who love to remove dryer lint through various wands and suction aids, et cetera.

You can even order a silver-toned toothpick holder engraved with your initials!

There's also a disproportionate number of afghans that insist on paying tribute to dogs, daughters-in-law, and even "like-a-sisters." There are all sorts of touching sentiments stitched into these, but they're a bit treacly for my taste. Call me cynical but I'd put this on the "like a sister" afghan just to see her flip out:

You hang around the house a lot
You stole from Uncle Jim
When he was in the crazy house
You claimed you were blood kin
But when he's gone to glory

And that final bell shall chime
Be advised you're not a sister
You ain't gettin' one thin dime.

Harsh? I know. My stuff will *so* never get into the Cracker Barrel holiday gift shop.

My favorite from the weirdo Christmas catalogs this year was the "Fanny Bank: Makes Saving Money a Real Gas!"

Just put money into the plastic plumber's butt crack and listen to six flatulent sound effects that get louder the more money you put in. Beats the hell out of the snoring fake dog, am I right?

As I sat rather smugly in the pew we had staked out a good half hour before the service, we had time to review which Christmas movies we'd watch that night.

Hubby's a traditionalist and favors the black-and-white version of *It's a Wonderful Life,* the dreary story of a do-gooder who gets depressed about his life, gets all likkered up, and wrecks his car.

"That makes it sound terrible when you describe it like that," says hubby, who begins to prattle on about the film's message of kindness and faith and friendship. While he talks, I continue to enjoy watching Muffy and Buffy slowly realize that they ain't getting in and will have to attend the dreaded "children's service" where they will be pelted with Goldfish crackers and snot for most of the hour.

Their children's "gawjus Crusmus sweatahs" don't stand a chance.

Soph votes for the real classic of the holiday: National Lampoon's *Christmas Vacation.* I could watch Chevy Chase get hit by that sliding attic staircase a zillion times and never get tired of it. Simply. The. Best.

Still, I'm feeling a little naughty, not nice, and I vote for *Bad Santa,* because Billy Bob Thornton, like Denzel, is just someone who never lets me down. I'll pay to see them in anything just for the joy of watching them. Billy Bob is probably the most unlikely movie star imaginable—a wormy, undistinguished little man who just, somehow, has "it." He could've probably made *It's a Wonderful Life* a good movie.

"*Bad Santa!* That's rated R!" says hubby, while, in my peripheral vision (which is practically bionic by the way), I saw the "sweatah" set finally huffing out the door of the narthex, apparently having been told that a roll of twenties wouldn't be enough to displace the sweet little widows in the front pew. Justice had been served; somewhere an angel was getting his wings.

My friend Nan doesn't cook often, but when she does, it's always delish. When Duh and I were newlyweds, we rented an apartment on the third floor of a beach house smack-dab between the Intracoastal Waterway and the Atlantic Ocean. The North Carolina Holiday Flotilla, held on the first Saturday after Thanksgiving every year, cruised right by our front porch on the waterway and we drank this wassail and watched the parade in the company of all of our rowdy friends. As any beach Bubba will tell you, "It don't get no better'n that."

Serve Nan's wassail in those cute snowman mugs you probably paid too much for at Pottery Barn last year.

NAN'S WASSAIL BOWL

6 cups apple cider (not juice)
1 large can pineapple juice
2 tablespoons honey
2 sticks cinnamon
1 orange with cloves stuck in it
Juice *and* grated zest of two lemons
Dark rum to taste

In a large pot over medium heat, combine everything but the rum and bring to a near boil. Keep on low and add the rum about a half hour before you're serving, stirring to mix. Ahhhhhh.

23

Sex Every Night for a Year? How Do You Wrap That?

As hubby and I approach our twentieth wedding anniversary this year, I'm grateful as hell that neither one of us suffers from a new ailment I just read about called hyperthymestic syndrome.

Who that, you say?

Well, picture this. What would it be like to remember every single event in your life, from the kind of cake you had at your third birthday party to how much you paid for a Grand Funk Railroad album? Life's highs and lows never forgotten because of HS, which is derived from the Greek words, "hyper" meaning "big pain" and "thymesis" meaning "in the ass."

Or close to that.

Only a few people in the world have HS but, luckily enough, one of them has just written a book and the other is the subject of one of those smart-person PBS-type documentaries that I usually try to avoid in favor of watching *Celebrity Rehab 2* on VH1.

I think it would be hard to be married to someone with HS.

She: "Hon, you didn't take the trash out."

He: "Yes, I did. Which reminds me. The first time I ever took the trash out was June 16, 1969. It was a sunny day with a thirty percent chance of rain. I ate an egg salad sandwich and Hawaiian Punch for lunch and rode bikes with Jimmy Moran from down the street until approximately 5:10 P.M."

She: "Fascinating. What do you think we should have for dinner tonight?"

He: "Hmmm. How 'bout you make the dinner you made on November 3, 2002?"

She: "A little help?"

He: "Duhhh. Marinated lamb shanks and buttered couscous, you silly woman. I swear, sometimes I think you'd forget your head if it wasn't attached to your shoulders."

She: "I was just thinking how funny you'd look with your head *not* attached to your shoulders. Hahahahahaha!"

He: "What?"

She: "Nothing."

With HS, you'd never have an excuse for forgetting special occasions.

He: "Are you kidding? Today's our anniversary?"

She: "Lemme get this straight. You can remember the

day in seventh grade when you bought new shoelaces for your gym shoes and you can't remember *the most important day of your life?*"

He: "Well, they were very nice shoelaces, and a steal at sixty-nine cents a pair and with tax, that made it . . ."

I hate to admit it, but if I had HS, I'd use my powers for evil.

Me: "You said you'd buy me one of those diamond necklaces with the yesterday, today, and tomorrow diamonds on it for our twentieth anniversary."

Duh: "When did I say that?"

Me: "March 20, 1992, and don't *even* argue with me about it or I will be forced to recall a certain August 16, 2004."

Duh: "I have no idea what happened that day."

Me: "That was the day that you said that, yes, as a matter of fact, my Capri pants did make me look fat."

Duh: (silent)

Me: "Psych! No you didn't! You are so lame!"

Having HS would kinda blow. You'd never be able to forget the tragic stuff in life: where you were when the Challenger blew up or when you learned that Denise Richards was going to star in her own reality show, for instance.

And you'd remember every bad decision (the vintage Audi), every disappointment (the last *Seinfeld* episode), every time you gave your heart to another only to realize they didn't even know you were alive (I'm talking to you, Mr. Jimmy Smits), every Low Moment in Parenting (Benadryl before Target trip equals peaceful shopping experience).

I had some more examples, but I forget 'em.

With the twentieth anniversary approaching, I'm casting about for unique gift ideas for hubby. The truth is, I love him madly and resent it just a little when he jokes that, if he dies first, I'll bring a date to the funeral.

"That's a terrible thing to say," I said, looking wounded. "It's not like I could get anybody good on such short notice, anyway."

In honor of our twentieth year, Duh has decided to grow a beard. This is the closest a man gets to having a pregnant stomach touched by strangers because everyone likes to touch a new beard, unless it's Michael Moore's, bless his heart. (And have you seen that creepy pregnant man? He has a beard *and* a pregnant belly so how do you know which to touch first?)

Everybody feels the need to comment on a new beard.

His mama: "Oh, son, you look just like Jesus himself with that beard."

His boss: "The guy with the cardboard 'will work for weed' sign down at the underpass."

The car salesman: "Oh, Jesus, definitely Jesus. With just a touch of Abraham Lincoln thrown in. Sir."

Me: "Tom Hanks in *Cast Away* right when he lost his mind and started yakking with a volleyball. At least I think it was a volleyball. It might've been a soccer ball. It was, like, some sort of sports thing and he made a face on it with his own blood. No, wait. Maybe it was fish blood. Hey! Did you take the garbage out tonight? No? Who do you think you are?

You're kidding. No, only your mama thinks that. OK, and the car salesman."

Looking for something more creative than the usual tool, book, CD, clothes, et cetera that I buy hubby for special occasions, I came across a story about what a Charlotte, North Carolina, woman did to mark her husband's fortieth birthday.

Charla Muller, mom of two and certified crazy person, told her husband that she would make love to him every day for one whole year. No matter what. No excuses.

Great. I'd finally decided to give the newly bearded hubby the DeWalt eighteen-volt cordless hammer drill *with* six-tool capacity, but now that seemed unspeakably unoriginal thanks to Charla.

Way to go, girlfriend. Thanks to all the publicity your big idea got, I'll probably have to throw in the radio-charger gizmo, too.

Duh read the article about Charla Muller one morning over breakfast. Until then, we were both perfectly happy to stick to the loving and emotionally committed plan to make sure that, at the very least, we'd do it on national holidays. This "Don't go knockin' if, uh, the banks are closed" system has become so well-known that my gal pals have actually apologized for calling after they realize, too late, that it's Presidents' Day.

But this? *This?* Every day for an entire year? Charla said in a newspaper interview that by the ninth month she'd hit "the proverbial wall."

"I felt like beating myself over the head with the nearest newspaper or maybe a spatula," she told a reporter.

Oh, girl, stop beating yourself up. Allow me to do that. Now, where did I put that cinder block?

Even nutty Dr. Oz says you should have sex about two hundred times a year. But then, he's always running off at the mouth about something that I think he just makes up in his head right before he goes on the air. Like the time he said on *Oprah* that your pee should be clear enough to read through (yuck) or that the perfect poo is shaped like an *S* (double yuck) and Oprah is, like, all excited, going "Nailed it!!!" (triple yuck, double word score, and Yahtzee!).

Charla said that she wanted to pick a gift that would be so special that her husband would never have to pause and wrack his brain to remember what she gave him for his fortieth.

If he ever does, she has my permission to, as we say in the South, "go upside his head."

Can you imagine him ever saying: "Honeypie, was it my fortieth birthday when I got mooney-gooney every day for a full year or was that the year you and the kids gave me the stainless-steel turkey smoker?"

When I first read about Charla's plan, I figured she was just desperate to find a gift that wouldn't have to be exchanged. I mean, one hopes.

There's no chance of regifting 365 nights of sex. It's not like he's going to say, "Hon, don't take this personally, but I think I'm just gonna give this to Tad in accounting; he's been a little depressed lately. . . ."

In a time when more and more married couples joke that they've been reduced to "hallway sex" (that's when you pass in the hall and she says "F-you" and he says "F-you" back), perhaps Charla's idea isn't all that terrible.

Then again, Omaha steaks are always nice.

There are tons of recipes for better-than-sex cake out there and most of them involve chocolate. My Duh prefers fruity spice cakes, so this has become the BTS cake of choice at our house.

BETTER-THAN-SEX-365-NIGHTS CAKE

3 cups flour

1 teaspoon soda

½ teaspoon salt

2 cups sugar

1 teaspoon cinnamon

3 eggs

¾ cup oil

1½ teaspoons vanilla extract

8 ounces pineapple (with juice)

1 cup pecans

1¾ cups mashed bananas

Combine flour, soda, salt, sugar, and cinnamon. Add eggs, oil, and vanilla. Stir 'til moist. Do not beat! Stir in pineapple and juice, pecans, and mashed bananas.

Pour batter into three 8-inch cake pans that have been greased and floured. Bake at 350 degrees for 25 minutes.

Frost layers when cool with this Nutty Cream Cheese Frosting: Beat together 'til fluffy one stick butter and 8 ounces cream cheese. Add a box of confectioner's sugar, 1 teaspoon vanilla, and half a cup of chopped pecans, and mix 'til it's good and spreadable.

24

Japanese Moms, Meet Most Honorable Uncrustables

The army is advancing, headed toward my street. From the looks of it, they'll be here in T-minus two minutes, spreading out, covering the left flank (Mrs. Hoolihan's yard) and the right (Mr. Ledbetter's). I'm busted. They've already seen me, water hose in hand, trying to coax a few last-minute blooms out of the periwinkle before the first frost.

At this point, the only way I can avoid the Cub Scouts selling popcorn to the east and the chorus students (including my own Princess!) peddling catalogs for everything from chocolate turtles to *Newsweek* to looks-sorta-like-silver necklaces to the west, is to lay down in the shrubbery and pretend to be dead.

Even then, the persistent school/scout sales team, none over five feet tall, will probably poke at my body just to make sure.

Can I really stand the chubby Cub Scout from down the

street, telling others, "Snap! She's not even cold yet; wish we'd gotten here a few minutes sooner. From the size of her, I'd guess she was good for at least a coupla pounds of coconut almond treasures."

Would the Princess look dejected and only muster a lame "She was alive when she made my lunch three hours ago"?

The scouts are selling popcorn and candy in tins roughly the size of a doghouse. Who needs that?

A flyer left in my door earlier in the day advised, "It's time to order your holiday popcorn!" I don't get the connection. The wise men brought gold, frankincense, and myrrh, not butter toffee, confetti, and "bedda cheddar."

Whatever. I can easily say no to strangers, even ones in uniform. And I can even say no to my mom friends who have torpedoed more than a few girls' nights out by covering the table—and displacing my yummy pear martini in the process—with an array of overpriced gift-wrap samples for their kids' school fund-raiser.

But saying no to the Princess is, naturally, much harder.

There are four catalogs to choose from, she chirps while fanning them out on the coffee table one night.

"Isn't-it-time-you-said-yes!-to-aromatic-oils" she begins in a stilted monotone, and I hold up my hand to stop her before she can add, "sir or madam."

"Don't need any."

But she has been trained, Navy SEAL–style, apparently, and failure is not an option.

"Dreidel salt and pepper shakers?"

"We're not Jewish."

"Caramel mittens and chocolate kittens gift set?"

"Gross."

"Lavender body mist?"

"Do I look ninety-five???"

"If I sell $500 worth of merchandise, I get a cool hamburger phone just like the one in *Juno*."

Great. My daughter's role model is a pregnant teenager who talks into a sesame-seed bun.

It almost made me nostalgic for when she launched a campaign for an iPhone. For me. Because she was mortified by the age of my uncool cell phone.

She would look at me with a mix of pity and frustration when I said that I was holding out for a cell phone that would wash the cat, cook a pizza in its tiny little guts, and even go to her dance recital so I wouldn't have to.

"Kidding!" I had said when her sweet little face fell, dumping the freckles right off it and onto the floor. "You know mommie knows it's unsafe to wash a cat."

"You're a dinosaur!" the Princess said. Her words were harsh but her expression was worse. I imagined it was the exact expression worn by Orville and Wilbur Wright when they were greeted by crowds wearing STEAM LOCOMOTIVES ROCK! T-shirts wherever they went.

"Yes, but a dinosaur who loves you enough to . . ." And with that, I won over the Princess and made her forget all about the hamburger phone and lavender body mist and all the rest of it.

I was going to take her to American Girl Place in New York City.

Which was way better than the hamburger phone, judging from her reaction.

Fast-forward one month and we're sitting in the American Girl Place Cafe, which is pink and gorgeous and offered a couple of surprises to this dinosaur.

For starters, the waiters are surprisingly hot. I halfway expected ours to place my Cobb salad in front of me and then, with a flourish, free himself of his breakaway shirt and pants, Chippendales style.

Second, you need to know about the chocolate mousse. It's served in a little green plastic flowerpot with a daisy stuck in the center and it's unbelievably delish. (Later that week, I even told the waiter at Bobby Flay's fancy restaurant that he should try to get their recipe and he looked faint.)

American Girl Place, all four levels of it, is a wonder. All day long, cabs disgorge mothers, doll-clutching daughters, and a few visibly horrified, red-faced little brothers at its doors. Not only is there a doll hair salon but also a doll hospital where destructive little girls from all over the East Coast take their Felicitys and Nellies to repair detached limbs or missing eyes. (The average "hospital" stay is two weeks, so at least they must have a great HMO.)

When the Princess and I realized she wouldn't be able to dine with her doll because the doll wouldn't be done with her hair appointment by then (seriously), a concerned, hot waiter escorted us to a veritable orphanage of loaner dolls. I had a brief *Bride of Chucky* moment (well, there were so *many* of them) before he positioned the freckled blonde we selected between us in a pink chair that clipped to the tabletop and fetched her a cup of tea. I felt a brief, nasty tug to say, "Dude, you do know this doll isn't real, right?"

We fussed over the doll until the mousse came.

"You're on your own, Toots," I mumbled between spoonfuls. The orphan seemed to frown.

On every table was a fancy little box of "icebreaker" questions. Ridiculous, this notion that I would need a cheat sheet to talk to my own daughter. But, uh, let's just say that now I know if Sophie could be any tree in the forest, I know which one she would be.

After lunch, we attended the American Girl musical revue, *Circle of Friends,* which was about, uh, a circle of friends, and contained many Wholesome Life Lessons that made me miss the waiters. Sorry. I like a little off-color cynicism after a big meal.

Sure American Girl Place was gimmicky and there were some dads there who looked about as happy as Lindsay Lohan at a Franklin Graham crusade, but generally it was a delight. Would we go back? Probably not, because now that the Princess is in middle school, she's aging out of doll land and into the world of middle-school monthly "dances," and talk of who's going with who, which, from what I can tell, is more a state of mind than actual fact.

Still, I'm glad we had the experience. Being a mom brings these profound moments when your heart is so full, and they come out of nowhere.

A walk down the baby products aisle at the drugstore will make your gut ache when you catch the scent of Johnson's baby powder. Whoa. Where did that come from?

I remember getting emotional when we went to a Hilary Duff concert, and it was the same way at American Girl Place. We'd always remember our day there but we wouldn't go back.

The mom-daughter moments won't always be nearly as sweet as talcum powder or swaying together with a glow stick in a concert hall or excitedly saving the plastic flower stuck in the mousse for a souvenir, but when it is, it's spectacular, y'all.

But even though I can be a bit of a mushpot over things involving the Princess, the moms who completely put their lives on hold for their kids mystify me.

The latest pain-in-the-ass trend is for moms to create little bento-box lunches for their children.

Now everybody knows Japanese mothers are crazy-san because they've been doing this stuff for years, getting up in the wee hours to carve a bird-of-paradise from a single carrot or whittle a cluster of radishes into the shape of a dragon.

American mommies consider it good enough to toss a couple of Uncrustables into a bag and pray that they thaw in time to be edible.

But now, the bento-box obsession is showing up in my kid's school. One mom I heard about cut up a boiled egg to look just like a daffodil; another carved a realistic bunny rabbit entirely out of white cheddar for her kid's bento box; another made faux sushi rolled from strawberry cream cheese, bananas, and white bread.

In Japan, the bento lunch box is highly competitive because mothers believe a successful bento box represents the "uprightness of the household and the true measure of a mother's love."

Baloney. And I mean just in the round sense, not whittled into the shape of the Jonas Brothers.

Great. I finally got the hang of making pancakes shaped like Mickey Mouse's head and now I gotta mold rice balls that look just like Hello Kitty for my kid's lunch box. Wonder if it's OK to substitute Sour Patch Kids candy for miniature fruit kebobs shaped like bees and dragonflies favored by some supermoms.

"Missy's mommie made macaroni-and-cheese shaped just like a VW beetle and she used lemon Fruit Roll-Ups for the windows," the Princess sulked one day as I tossed a bag of cheese-type-product-flavored Doritos into her plain insulated lunch bag from Target.

"Missy's mommie sounds like she needs several months of intense psychotherapy," I said cheerfully. "Uh. Don't mention to anyone that I said that."

In Japan, the bento-box craze is as competitive as cheerleading in Texas. Like I was saying, the idea is rooted in a centuries-old belief that a properly made bento box sent to school reminds the child that he is cherished and his home is a safe haven. Even as he is biting into a train caboose made entirely of whittled sea urchin, his mother is literally counting the minutes until his return home. Nah, that won't give him a complex.

Far be it from me to criticize another culture's ancient beliefs. Kidding! Of course that's what I'm doing but it's for all the right reasons: American mommies have enough crap to do without fretting about our kid having Most Honorable Lunch Box. We have gift wrap to buy; pilgrimages to fancy, overpriced doll stores to make. When will it ever be enough?

On the other hand, I'm not terribly worried that this bento-box craze will take hold in the South for very long. It's damned near impossible to make a decent Dora the Explorer out of potted meat.

Here's a great reason to avoid buying your kid a bento box. The little compartments are too small to properly contain these amazing cookies, made by my mother-in-law, Nancy, for her grandchildren since they were old enough to chew. They're ridiculously crisp and buttery and take a bit of time to master but you're smart (else you wouldn't have bought this book or associated yourself with someone who did) and I have great faith you can do it. When you do master them, be sure to mail me some so I can let you know how they stack up. I know some of you are getting all nervous because of the two sticks of butter but, hell, that's just the morning toast allotment for Paula Deen, and everybody loves her cooking. Besides, the oatmeal balances everything out, am I right?

FABULOUS OATMEAL CRISPIES

2 sticks butter
1 cup *each* white and brown sugar
2 eggs, beaten
1 teaspoon vanilla extract
1½ cups flour
1 teaspoon *each* baking soda and salt
1 cup finely chopped nuts (any type of nut will do)
3 cups oatmeal

Cream butter and sugars; add eggs and vanilla. Set aside. Sift together flour, baking soda, and salt and add to egg mixture. Fold in nuts and oatmeal and mix 'til everything's smooth. Form into a roll the size of those store-bought refrigerated cookies. Wrap the roll in wax paper and refrigerate until the dough is firm enough to slice. Using sharp knife, slice 1/4-inch wide (more or less) cookies and place on cookie sheet. Bake at 325 degrees until lightly brown (about 12 minutes). Remove from pan and cool on wire rack.

They'll stay fresh in an airtight container for a week or so, although we've never tested that theory. Nancy usually gives us a big Ziploc bag of 'em to take home from our Christmas visit to her house four hours away and they don't even last half the drive.

25

Strapped for Cash?
Try Cat Whisperin'

We didn't decorate for Halloween this year, at least not in the traditional way, with cardboard skeletons and red-eyed bats taped to the front door. No, when the kids trick-or-treated at our house, all they saw was the crumpled and tear-stained third-quarter statement for our 401-Kaput tacked up there.

And while most kids were oblivious enough to say, "Huh?", their helicopter parents got the message and shuddered visibly in the shadows.

When I opened the last statement, I jumped out of the window. True, it was the kitchen window and I only fell two feet, so the whole scene lacked drama, but I thought that was the required reaction to extreme financial turmoil in America. And I am nothing if not patriotic.

The economy being in the tank is affecting all of us. At

our monthly girls' night out, we split overpriced entrees and asked for, count 'em, three free breadbaskets. One of my more well-heeled friends was particularly despondent as she looked sorrowfully into her empty glass of "house" Chardonnay.

"I got my hair cut at Supercuts today," Claire whispered.

"Was he at least gay?" asked another former rich girl.

Claire sobbed. "He wasn't even a he. He was a she. And all she wanted to do was talk about how her kid made a picture of a turkey for Thanksgiving by outlining his palm for the turkey's body and his fingers for the turkey's feathers and it won a *prize*. When Rafiki did my hair, it was like a floor show, all those spats with that diva Fernando, who was always leaving to go get another bro-zilian wax. The sexual tension was overwhelming. And she thinks her kid's the first one to trace a turkey out of his hand. What an idiot!"

Since I'm the only one in the group whose kid goes to public school *and* who doesn't belong to a country club, I was feeling a little flush by comparison.

That's the beauty of being a redneck at heart. We tend to live *below* our means because we're always terrified that somebody's going to take away what we have.

This year, the economy was way scarier than any Jaycees haunted house or neighborhood party with obligatory bowls of grape "eyeballs" and spaghetti "intestines." That's child's play. The truth was that these quarterly statements couldn't be any more frightening if T. Rowe Price himself delivered them inside Alan Greenspan's severed head. Which a few bitter folks wouldn't mind so much.

The only good news is that trend watchers say that being frugal is actually hip these days. If you drink Starbucks instead of McDonald's coffee, you might find yourself getting the same sneer that, just a year ago, was reserved for people who drove Hummers.

Funny how much difference a year makes. The same folks who kvetched about the lousy job their undocumented housekeeper did on dusting the ceiling fan blades now squeal excitedly, "Ooooh! I think I have a coupon for a free appetizer!" when they go out to eat, and then proceed to dump the contents of their Dooney & Bourkes onto the table at Ruby Tuesday.

And just recently I overheard a venerable old country-club snoot huff at the grocery store clerk: "Excuse me, my dear, but I am quite certain that Tide detergent is a bogo."

Financial experts say we shouldn't panic-sell stock because this, too, shall pass. They explain all this in terms of "bulls" and "bears," with bull markets being good and bear markets being trying to figure out how to comfortably sit on the bus while wearing a barrel and suspenders. Call it the recessionista look.

Thankfully, the experts say that due to the cyclical nature of the stock market, we should expect to return to a prosperous "bull" market in, say, anywhere from eighteen months to twenty-four years. The world's greatest economists have boldly predicted that, basically, this whole recession/ depression thing is "gonna hang around like a fart in a hot shower." Or words to that effect.

Discussing all this with duh-hubby, we've decided that, as our piddlin' investments disappear faster than a bag of weed at a Cypress Hill concert, we should consider augmenting our income in creative ways. Frankly, I'd like to be the new new host of *The Price Is Right,* for instance. The whole Drew Carey thing isn't working out; he looks antsy. Could they have found anyone less well-suited for that gig? Oh, right. Out-of-work former veep Dick ("Dick") Cheney. I could see him trying to pop a cap into an overly excited mom from Peoria who correctly guessed the price of Turtle Wax ("Shut up, you squealing cow!").

Duh and I are inspired by the creative way the rich get richer. Did you know, for instance, that Jennifer Lopez got paid $1.2 million to sing "Happy Birthday" at some old billionaire's party? Or that Justin Timberlake will drop by your party for $200,000 and, if you pay $700,000 more, he'll sing to you?

So what? So this. We live in a world where it's conceivable that even Z-listers like Gary Coleman could make a grand for simply showing up at a party, rolling his eyes and saying, "Whatchu talkin' 'bout, Willis?"

I don't blame 'em. I say get it while you can, because fame is fickle. Pete Rose can't even get twenty bucks for an autograph these days. And remember Anna Nicole Smith's whatever-he-was, Howard K. Stern? His celebrity status rivals that of the guy who used to play the blind girl's husband on *Little House on the Prairie.*

You can probably see where I'm headed with this. As a card-carrying Z-lister my own self, I'll show up at your birthday party, hog killin', bris, shrimp-a-roo, chicken bog, cockfight, or chili cook-off for, let's say, $29.99. I can't sing, of course, but I can juggle fire batons. OK, not really, but I saw it on *America's Got Talent* one time, and how hard can it be?

You're not feelin' me?

OK, how about this—I'm going to become a cat whisperer. It pays better and I know I'd be good at it.

And, yes, I said cat whisperer.

Someone who counsels your cat.

Over the phone.

And claims to understand what the cat is thinking.

Duh and I researched this as a possible moneymaker and, turns out people who are otherwise able to feed and dress themselves and act normally will pay up to $300 to a long-distance cat whisperer.

The cat doesn't actually hold the phone to its flappy little ear; that would be weird. Rather, the owner of the cat submits a photo of the cat that needs a good whisperin', if you will, and later, during the human-to-human call, the cat sits nearby.

Laughing hysterically, I'm guessing.

This is the silliest thing I've heard since the cat yoga craze a couple of years ago. I went right out and bought a cat yoga instruction book and tiny terry-cloth headband and renamed my girl cat "Olivia Neutered John," which she didn't think was funny. Cats have no sense of irony.

But they do have vocabularies, according to the cat whisperer who told the Associated Press reporter that one of her cats was unhappy because his food tasted "just like sawdust." That's right: "Cats have normal vocabularies," said the whisperer.

Who knew? Wonder if they can define "scam"?

Here's the thing. I have two enormous house cats curled around my bare feet at this very moment and I can tell you that they don't know sawdust from Shinola.

But if their dumbass owners will pay me to say different, then I'll do what it takes to stay outta that barrel on the bus.

In one case, said the cat whisperer interviewed, the client's cat was upset that she was ignoring him in favor of a younger cat living in the home.

No Shinola!

Cats are notoriously jealous creatures. But the owner bought into this theory completely and used big, human-sized words to describe her shame at having "marginalized" the difficult kitty.

The cat, having heard a promise for "less marginalizing" was heard to think, *I say, that's marvelous news indeed. But in other, more pressing matters, do you believe that we can actually sustain a fifty percent reduction in worldwide greenhouse gas emissions by 2050 or is the G8's goal merely a meaningless compromise that would actually do very little to stop global warming?*

See how good I whisper?

The reporter admitted to being skeptical at first but, after getting her own cat whispered, she did stop her compulsive licking (the cat, not the reporter, although I did once share a cubicle with a reporter who compulsively smelled her own feet) after just one session and the other cat no longer sticks her face into the other cat's ass.

Baby steps, y'all.

Cat whisperers are paid all this money to read the cat's minds and you don't even have to leave the comfort of your own home! You could be one of those freaky 740-pound women who pays the misfit neighbor kid to bring her pizza every hour on the hour and still make money at this. Hey, it beats the living hell out of working the fourth-meal nightshift at Taco Bell, am I right?

I've had cats all my life, so I'm just as qualified to "whisper" as the next person. Plus, I believe we've all established that, unless I want to keep dividing entrees and cutting my own bangs, I'm going to have to generate some extra scratch.

I just this minute did a little test run on my own two fur "slippers" still curled around my feet and snoring loudly.

"Do you think a human can read your mind?" I whispered.

One yawned and stretched and the other, uh, yawned and stretched. I think they're saying they're "tired."

I got the gift! Let the whisperin' begin.

Here's a budget-conscious recipe for the current economic climate that Duh and the Princess just love. Added benefit:

You can give the drained tuna juice to the cats and they'll whisper loving thoughts back to you. I swear.

"YOU AIN'T TOO GOOD TO EAT THIS" TUNA NOODLE CASSEROLE

1 large can tuna (drain and pour juice into cat's bowl)
½ cup *each* chopped celery and onion, sautéed 'til translucent
2 cups shredded cheddar cheese
1 can cream of celery soup
½ cup mayonnaise
½ cup milk
8–12 ounces wide or curly egg noodles, cooked

Mix all that together and pour into a greased casserole dish that's big enough to hold it all. Sprinkle with bread crumbs. (Make your own from Wonder Bread; your fancy-ass Panko crumb days are over.) Bake at 350 degrees 'til bubbly, about 30 minutes. Serve with hopes for a brighter future.

Mamas, Don't Let Your Sons Grow Up to Be Cheaters

My pick for the best quote of the year comes from the Australian woman Anna Warrick, who was asked to comment on one little town in the Outback's attempt to boost the female population by, essentially, recruiting ugly women.

The mayor of Mount Isa got in deep roo-doo after telling the newspaper that women of the, er, homely persuasion should consider moving to his town because Mount Isa men aren't all that picky.

There was also a ham-handed reference to just how grateful these women appear to be once given the attentions of a Mount Isa man.

But it was Anna Warrick who noted that there aren't a lot of gems to be found among the town's men, either: "We have a saying up here that the odds are good, but the goods are odd."

Amen, sistah.

Perhaps the oddest is Hizzoner John Molony, who told the newspaper, "May I suggest if there are five blokes to every girl, we should find out where there are beauty-disadvantaged women and ask them to proceed to Mount Isa."

Recruit ugly women, in other words. 'Cause we all know how grateful they are.

Unable to stop himself, Mayor McCheese added his personal observation that, "Quite often you will see walking down the street a lass who is not so attractive with a wide smile on her face. Whether it is recollection of something previous or anticipation for the next evening, there is a degree of happiness."

That's right. Mae-Jean's gon' get some on her—at least that's the way it sounded.

The mayor is like the clueless husband who buys his wife a steam iron for her birthday and then wonders why she spends the day weeping behind a locked bedroom door.

Because Google is a wonderful thing, I was able to satisfy my own curiosity as to what this mayor looked like, this man who would judge other people's beauty with such confidence.

Would he have the rugged good looks of Mel Gibson? Or would he more closely resemble the talented and handsome Heath Ledger, who left us way too soon? Or would the mayor possess the more sensitive, even delicate, features of that cerebral Aussie country singer Keith Urban?

Nope. He's pretty much Fred Flintstone. The goods are, well, odd, just as Anna said.

The mayor had to start backpedaling when his comments got out and he had to apologize for dishing up a big bowl of wrong to the women of Mount Isa. The next time he encounters "a lass who is not so attractive with a wide smile on her face" I'd bet that smile has nothing to do with her envisioning that night's steamy encounter in the sack with one of Mount Isa's menfolk, but instead she's probably picturing tossing the mayor into the eager jowls of a wild dingo.

What *is* it with men, anyway?

Hons, I have to tell you that I was crushed at the revelation that my former political crush, John Edwards, had strayed.

My attractive, single friend Susie quipped over a glass of wine when the news leaked that she was upset about Edwards' cheating heart for two reasons.

"On the one hand, it's just so horribly disappointing that he's that kind of man," she said, "but on the other hand, I'm upset because all this time I didn't know he was available."

Awful, but funny, right? Edwards was my U.S. senator when I bumped into him at the post office and was too starstruck to even manage a "howdy."

His impossibly boyish good looks and earnest antipoverty speeches were as intoxicating as a Limoncello mojito, which they drink a lot of in Beverly Hills, where John Edwards visited his mistress and their "love baby," if the *National Enquirer* can be believed. Which, I think, it can.

Mainstream media: You snoozed and loozed while the Edwards scandal was broken by the same supermarket tabloid that reported that Barack Obama's stepmother likes to talk to the ghost of Elvis (as if he were really dead) *and,* doing the math here, that exercise-addicted Kelly Ripa now officially weighs less than my left thigh.

I miss reading the *Enquirer* at the beauty parlor because now it's gone upscale and calls itself a "sah-lon" and took away the *Enquirer* and even *Weekly World News*, with its interviews with wolf-faced little girls and whatnot. Now it's all chichi with French *Vogue* and a bunch of other high-fashion stuff that doesn't tell me a damn thing about the important events unfolding in the world, like Edwards' dalliance or how a cat walked across the country three thousand miles to reunite with its owner. French *Vogue* wouldn't know a good story if it bit its entire editorial staff on the ass, but then I'm guessing it would be almost impossible to find any ass on those models and their handlers.

Time was, I wouldn't have believed anything in the *Enquirer.* Sure, it was fun to read; who can honestly resist a good story about a child who is born half boy and half bat or somesuch. No one I ever want to know, that's who.

But exposing my former favorite millworker's son as a womanizer bedding a rather horse-faced hoochie while his wife battled cancer has changed all that.

Now I am, to use poker parlance, "all in" with the *Enquirer.*

Sure, they pay their sources and their sources are often anonymous and perhaps spend their days walking outdoors behind shopping carts, but even a blind squirrel finds a nut every now and then.

This time the nut was Edwards, who must've been nervously pulling out the very $400 coiffure I had defended to the point of needing bed rest, as he wondered just how the hell his forty-four-year-old girlfriend got pregnant.

I mean, I know *how* she got pregnant, it's just that, don't you imagine Edwards thought that was one thing he didn't have to think about? (She said she was forty, she looked like she was forty-eight. . . .)

Having supported Edwards' various campaigns on state and national levels for years, I just hoped that he was the real deal. I ate up that "two Americas" stuff like a plate of cinnamon pancakes at the IHOP.

Which, now that I think about, might be as close as Edwards ever gets to international involvement for a while.

The one positive is to realize that, now that the *Enquirer* has broken a real story, I no longer have to feel the least bit self-conscious about reading anything in the little tabloid newspaper that has ads in the back for "removing evil spirit curses." I repeat: all in.

Edwards was just the most recent bad boy. Men are simple creatures and easily distracted by the new and bleached.

Because in my muddled noggin all roads lead back to TV

at some point, it makes me remember the *Trading Spaces* fiasco when the network suits fired perky Paige Davis.

Discarded by her corporate "boyfriends," Paige made 'em crawl back to her by doing nothing more than watching them fall flat without her.

After a couple of seasons of low ratings, even the suits admitted they'd been jerks.

"We felt like the bad boyfriend who had dumped her at the prom and now we're asking for a second chance," said one.

To fire Paige, they had even used that tired old excuse: "We just felt that we needed to go in a different direction."

How many times you heard that one, sistahs?

TV Guide coyly noted that the search for a new direction was answered when the show went "straight down the ratings tubes."

Oh, yes, they also "needed space." It was "not you, it's us." Whatever they said, it meant that loyal Paige, whose skill at using really big and dangerous power tools should've caused them some concern, was tossed like a used paint-tray liner.

But that was then and this is now and the scummy exboyfriend begged pitifully for a second chance.

While I personally think Paige should've let them twist in the wind, like Frank's homemade kitty-cat chimes, a bit longer, she's just too damn nice and perky for that, bless her heart.

So she said, "OK" and only asked that her best designer-friends (Hildi, Frank, Laurie, and Doug) be given the spotlight, too.

Paige has scored a win for all of us who have been, at some point in life, cast aside by the one we were loyal to in the search for someone "prettier" or "thinner" or "smarter" or "less-likely-to-stab-you-in-the-retina-if-you-cheat-on-her."

The good girl won when the bad boys who dumped her showed up—nervously twisting the latest lousy Nielsen ratings in their sweaty hands—and said they were sorry and would do anything to get her back.

Anything, that is, except letting Hildi plant grass on their office walls. Everybody's got limits, y'all.

Has your heart been broken or maybe just bent up a little? The ultimate indulgent comfort dessert is close at hand. Like all my favorite go-to recipes, this one is ridiculously easy but doesn't taste that way.

"YOU BROKE MY HEART SO I BUSTED YOUR JAW" APPLE ENCHILADAS

> 1 (21-ounce) can apple pie filling
> 6 (8-inch) flour tortillas
> 1 teaspoon cinnamon
> 1 stick butter
> ½ cup sugar

½ cup light brown sugar

1 pint vanilla ice cream (I prefer Ben & Jerry's)

Spoon pie filling evenly down the center of each torti-lla. Sprinkle with cinnamon; roll up, placing seam side down in lightly greased 9 × 13–inch baking dish.

Bring butter, sugars, and 1/2 cup water to a boil. Reduce heat and simmer, stirring constantly, for about 3 minutes. Pour over enchiladas. Let stand at least 30 minutes so it can soak in good. Bake at 350 degrees for 20 minutes. Serve hot, topped with a scoop or two of vanilla ice cream. Cheers up six despondent gal pals.

Epilogue

The Future Is Bloody Well Decided—Or Is It?

had just finished the book tour for the hardcover edition of *Belle Weather: Mostly Sunny with a Chance of Scattered Hissy Fits,* when it hit me: Vampires sell. Every store was full of promotional posters and displays of bestselling vampire lit. I could've sworn the salesclerk at Barnes & Noble said, "Neck, please." Face it: You can't sling a cat without hitting a vampire book these days.

The bad news is that I don't write about vampires. But, hons, that's all about to change. Maybe.

I got the idea from the Princess, who joined me for a road trip to Richmond, Virginia, the last stop on the *Belle Weather* tour. Her eleven-year-old nose was buried in the book for most of our five-hour drive.

Oh, not *my* book. Noooooo. She was reading something

called *New Moon,* which is the second book in a vampire series called *Twilight.*

"I thought you were going to read *my* book," I said, biting my lower lip and sounding utterly peevish.

"I am," she said, still not looking up. "And really soon. But I just can't put this thing down."

"Gimme that," I said, reaching out to grab the silly vampire book out of her hands and careening a little off the highway in the process.

"Hmmm," I said, scanning the jacket copy. This sounded pretty good. Mousy high school student Bella falls for dashing and devoted classmate Edward. What could go wrong?

Oh. He's a vampire. Well, that sucks.

The *Twilight* series has sold in the millions, mostly to preteen and teenage girls and their moms, who love them because the devout Mormon author makes it clear that Bella and Edward are saving themselves for marriage.

These moms are addicted to the vampire series, apparently because they don't understand that humorous nonfiction is what can really make their lives more fulfilling and interesting. No, what I meant to say is that they are giddy at the books' chaste message. It's almost as if they wouldn't mind it so much if their daughters would turn eighteen and, like Bella, get engaged to the supernice vampire boy from down the street.

The notion that any eighteen-year-old is thinking about marriage is scarier than a roomful of thirsty you-know-whats to me, but I can't fight it any longer: Vampires sell and I want in.

Sure, it'll be a little difficult at first because I write Southern-style humor, but I'm sure I can get the hang of it. Hell, how hard can it be?

So here's the plan: I'll create a main character, Bubba Bloodworth, a dashing, bib-overall-wearing vampire who brings a whole new meaning to the word "redneck."

Bubba's victims will be recruited as he cruises local tractor pulls, chicken bogs, and monster truck rallies, looking for, ahem, blood relations.

Beautiful women will willingly offer up their necks, unable to resist Bubba Bloodworth's signature pickup line: "Are you from Tennessee, 'cause you're the only ten I see."

Are you hooked yet? See, it'll be a whole subgenre, as we say in the publishing biz, the irresistible bumpkin-vampire who uses his considerable charms to lure women to his (corn) crib.

"Girl, you're hotter'n fish grease," Bubba Bloodworth will whisper seductively into his Southern belle victim's ear, causing her to giggle and squeal, "Oh, Bubba! You are just a vampire caution!"

If the vampire thing doesn't work out, I will go to Plan B which, based again on my tour of many bookstores throughout several states, is to write a book about a cat who lives in a library. And yes, of course, I know that's been done, but imitation is the sincerest form of plagiarism and mine would be a *vampire* cat if need be.

I told all this to the Princess on the drive home from Richmond but she didn't bite, so to speak.

"Mommie, you gotta stay true to yourself," she said. "You can't just suddenly start writing about vampires, even ones named Bubba."

"Vampire pussycat?"

"That doesn't even make any sense."

I pretended to agree with her, the same way I didn't argue when she said that Joe Jonas was the cutest of the Jonas Brothers. Any wise parent knows that, particularly at this tender cusp-of-teendom age, it's important to pick one's battles carefully.

"We'll see," I said, turning off I-95 as the sun set over an especially breathtaking field of cotton and we headed toward home. "We'll just see about that."

Acknowledgments

I am deeply grateful to these editors who have offered solid advice, unflagging support, gentle correction, and a steady paycheck over the years: Sammie Carter, Martie Proffitt, Bobby Parker, Dave Ennis, and Gwen Fowler from newspaperland, and the divine Jennifer Enderlin at St. Martin's Press.

I'm also grateful to my simply smashing literary agent, Jenny Bent. I am now, and always will be, Lana-Turner-discovered-at-the-soda-fountain lucky that she found me.

Thanks also to David High, a very brave and very funny Southern gentleman who knows all about "Crusmus sweatahs."

And, finally, long overdue and heartfelt thanks to Trey Wyatt, my former personal trainer, current comic inspiration, and one of the five people I hope to meet in heaven. Just not any time real soon.